Parables

OF A

PARAMEDIC

THOMAS VALENTINI

Parables of a Paramedic

© 2021, Thomas Valentini.

Print ISBN: 978-1-09837-2-378
eBook ISBN: 978-1-09837-2-385

CONTENTS

PREFACE

In the fall of 2012, I cleaned out my basement and sat in front of a pile of old cardboard boxes, as I had done every year since I began working as a paramedic. There were thousands of copies of patient care report (PCR) narratives I had made; usually in the ambulance in the middle of the night, after we finished emergency runs in the small city where I worked. Why on earth did I save these? I would sift through these and the memories would come flooding back—the faces, the battles they were fighting, how I tried to help them. There were some saves and success, but much suffering and death. I wanted to write a book that made some sense of these experiences, but I didn't want to resurrect the nightmares along with it.

As I read over the reports and my notes, I began to discover a pattern, but it was not what I expected. I found my comments often recalled the patients' faith and my recognition that the spirit of these individuals who fought for their lives was what motivated me to help them. The reason I could not give up as a medic was becoming clear. So, I began to write.

Herein is my chronicle of what we as healthcare providers are really up against: disease, trauma, pathophysiology, aging, social ills, moral and ethical degradation, a broken health care system, neglect, ourselves, and the unseen. The only way to win against all of this is to find common ground and work together.

While I try to be a good Christian, it has not been the sole lens through which I experienced my work or interactions with patients and colleagues. Over the course of decades of helping thousands of people of all faiths my eyes were opened to the common values and mission we all share. Like the parable of the Good Samaritan, a medic can take care of thousands on the road, not just one.

It took over thirty years and thousands of patients for me to learn what I could not see, and only then could I put that in writing.

Everything in this book is true and informed by my own notes and copied narratives I kept in a journal. I worked most of my career in Western Massachusetts but have worked across the state, a little in Connecticut and New York. I don't claim to have all the solutions—or the desire—to replace a system that has developed well in some clinical areas. What a medic can do in a moment for their patient can be routine, innovative, miraculous, or just a waste of time. Performing our job is not always about what skill or how we use it, but why we do it that answers the question of why it works.

In this book, I have tried to focus on the most relevant experiences to share with you and what they might mean to patients, their families, and the future of EMS. I've selected the experiences that were most poignant for me, but it's just a snapshot. I tried to do this in context the day-to-day job, which is far different from the televised portrayal in which a paramedic's job is to experience others suffering as their own personal roller coaster ride. These are not "war stories" nor partner relationships from a two-year tour. I won't waste our time with them.

We have been entrusted with the opportunity to help those who are ill and suffering, an opportunity that should be respected. With this occupation, there is a lot of insanity mixed with stupidity (the common culture of today), but we must rise above that to focus on those patients whose lives we have truly impacted and the much deeper inspirations that arise from these events. That is something to write about.

As for the spirituality and religion in this book, I make no claims, preach not and honestly try to be objective. As for the presence of both, I do believe they are *the single most important observation of all*. That was not the original focus of my writing thirty-four years ago; many of my notes were about the medications and procedures that did or didn't work. I find my experience is different not only because of the continuity from thousands of diverse circumstances over many years but because my approach was unbiased. I sought more of the scientific and medicinal solutions as I was taught in school. While transcribing the facts of these experiences into a narrative, a spiritual and soulful aspect came to light and cannot be ignored. Among the many questions I try to answer is *can the medical community's faith in science and technology work together with our patients spiritual and religious faith? Will my own faith endure and what can I learn from others? And can I work with another person's faith to help them?*

2 May 1986. Springfield MA: Patient with seizures. This is our seventh 911 call and only several hours into our shift. I swing out of the passenger's seat of the old Ford ambulance in front of the house for the seizure patient. I received my Basic EMT Certification card, and begun my job as an emergency medical technician (EMT). The first call was an allergic reaction with an obstructed airway. I am learning on the job with an experienced medic who knows his work. He grabs the cardiac monitor and I heave the large bag of supplies and oxygen over my shoulder and up the front porch stairs of the Victorian home.

"Pedi Seizures?" I ask. "That's the call." He replies in a matter-of-fact tone knowing most of the dispatched call natures have been wrong today.

The mother steps toward us with her infant cradled and the medic grasps the rigid, tremoring child from her arms over to the kitchen sink. We watch as he pulls off the child's shirt with one hand, wets the shirt with cool water from the tap and easily baths the child on his forearm over the sink with the cool water.

"He is hot, what's his temp mom? 102?" He asks and the mother nods.

"He's had Tylenol." She adds. "Has it stopped? He looks better."

The child's body slowly relaxes and without any medication appears to be over the seizure. The medic listens intently to the patient and the mother talk about the event simultaneously, reassuring her as I gather the child's meds and our gear. He strides down the six stairs in three steps and into the ambulance in two with child in his arm like a football and mom following. Care continues: assess, oxygen, monitor and a routine of care flows within two minutes. All is in order.

Our day flowed predictably as the diesel ambulance rumbled across town. We assessed each problem and resolved them one by one. I hauled the heavy bags of gear and patients with ease. The medic listened and interpreted what each patient needed, resolving concern or worry.

My goal was to help some people like my brother who suffered terrible seizures. Every job I had before this one was in vain. In this endeavor, I could do some good for those who needed good work done. I drove past the rows of identical houses in a blur and thought of when I was there for my brother. As a driving force, he was the reason I was here, my inspiration for helping the sickest get through their worst moments in life when no one else was there.

HE'S NOT HEAVY,
HE'S MY BROTHER.

22 September 1974. Hometown, Massachusetts. His eyes gaze off in the distance then roll back as his muscles become rigid with the sustained contractions of a seizure. I am about eleven years old, sitting by the bay window at home, holding my nine-year old brother. He only weighs about fifty pounds given his condition of Cerebral Palsy, scoliosis, developmental delays, para-seizures and constant illness. His seizure type activity is referred to as "spells" at the time because the doctors did not know what else to call them—or really what they are. What is known was that these are punishing episodes with extreme tonic spasm, muscle hyper-rigidity, and obvious pain and discomfort. They are "partial" in that he would not lose consciousness. I am taking care of him at home alone while my mom is grocery shopping. Of course, there are no cell phones in 1974. Back then we didn't call 911 either, like people do today; you had to be dying for one of those responses.

I know Doug has valium tablets in his bureau drawer, but I am afraid to give him one in case he chokes on it. Having seen these episodes many times before, I know we have to just wait it out until it ceases or subsides. All I can do is watch and wait. Looking down the street I can see my neighborhood friends playing tag football in the yard two houses down. I think how we should be out there just playing ball.

I count the seconds between his breaths knowing if it is more than ten, I need to breath for him, the thought of which makes me tremble. My fingers on his wrist, I count thirty-give pulsations in about fifteen seconds—140 a minute I guess; mine is probably the same. *What do I do? Why is this happening to him? Can I do the breathing thing over his mouth right? If I do it wrong will everyone be mad at me? Should I call and get help?*

I recall those moments, hammered as they are into my mind, and I don't know where I got the strength. I always managed the situation and carried my brother through it all—though I didn't have the prescience to realize that at the time.

The seconds tick by slowly. Seconds pass very slowly when you are in a desperate situation. *Seconds can seem an infinity.* One-one-thou-sand, two-one-thou-sand, three-one-thou-sand... They seem to go on and on, especially if someone is suffering or dying, suspended in time. Sounds seem quieted. It can be agonizing and seemingly pointless, but you know there is a loud point being made in that silence. Often during these moments, you tend to either not think at all or think deeply, intensely analyzing and contemplating, paralyzed but learning in that time.

My childhood home was in reality my training ground to become a competent and compassionate paramedic. I wish it wasn't because I would not want my brother to suffer for any reason. My love for my brother gave me the patience and drive to learn everything I needed to know to handle his care on my own at a young age, or help my folks. There were no visiting nurses or group homes; we cared for Doug at home around the clock. I had to learn basic care skills: how to carry, handle, and change his position when we learned he couldn't for himself; how to feed him by mouth years before his gastric feeding tube was implanted; how to apply his molded thoracic brace to keep his spine positioned well; how to make adjustments to his wheelchair for comfort and secure him in a van for transport; how to help administer his medicine followed by bland foods; and most of all how to provide emotional and spiritual support. It was a list of daily chores that required a nurturing and positive attitude. I thought some guys might think this was not "man's work." But it took a man-sized attitude to put my pride aside, along with activities my friends could do, like ride my dirt bike or play football so that I could keep Doug safe at home. I've applied that same attitude to my life's work. I tried to chronicle my work with him and his friends who were cared for years later at his group home, hoping that one day all brothers will rise up and care for their brothers as I did.

Not all medics think and feel the same way. As with any profession, there is a range in motivation and experience. In fact, most medics I've worked with don't think, see, or understand their patients or job like I do at all. Many see it as "just a job" or a steppingstone towards something else. They work robotically in hopes of achieving some other goal, usually motivated by money and comfort and the perception of less work. They say, "I really want to be a fire fighter, better money and benefits," or a cop, nurse, PA, doctor, teacher, pharmaceutical salesman, psychologist, an astronaut? Some want the nameplate with the string of initialized certifications and degrees after their name (Col. Thomas the 111, AS, BS, EMT-P, MBSA, VIP.) I ask them, so you want to work as a medic now, but would you want someone working on your loved one who doesn't like medicine or want to be there? Someone whose sole goal is to sit at a desk and do as little as possible? Pathetic, why bother. In my experience in several EMS systems, that's the majority and they give the rest of us a bad reputation, and it is one reason pre-hospital care has not advanced nearly as much as it should have.

Wherever needed, there are those few medics I have been fortunate to work with. They are as committed to the cause as I and have fought the good fight while dealing with tons of nonsense almost too lengthy to list. Some such medics might not look like the city's finest, with pressed uniforms, medals, and gold bling decorating their shirts. Some have big career aspirations but most just want to do their job for the patient and go home. These few are usually quiet and reserved by nature: head down, cap visor low. They prefer to blend in, work nights and weekends; that's often when we get our best work done. When hell breaks loose, they will be there on scene.

My younger brother and I were born in Springfield, Massachusetts and raised in a small, idyllic suburb nearby. My Mom and Dad worked extra hard to keep my brother at home. By this I mean the group home concept had not yet developed, and many kids like my brother were institutionalized at the Belchertown State School. That was a massive, low-level care facility for the mentally challenged who were often abandoned there with no family support. It was like a small prison: staff fed, medicated, neglected them and eventually buried the dead in the back yard. It housed twice its capacity by the time it closed in the 1990's.

Our family was not going to leave my brother there to fend for himself while we lived our lives in ignorance. I am very proud to say my folks never considered it, and we kept my brother at home, caring for him around the clock with practically zero outside help for over sixteen years. Trying circumstances can make even the closest of friends fade away, perhaps because they are simply busy with their own lives. This resulted in a degree of isolation, but that just made us stronger and drove us to be better care providers.

My mom and dad showed me what real strength was—and it was not what was portrayed at school or on television. My brother was very difficult to care for as he became older. He had episodes of illness and discomfort that ranged from the extreme physical with multiple surgeries to the mental para-seizure type activity. The frustration my parents endured, that we all endured, having to be up all hours every night took tremendous patience, strength, empathy, and dedication. These words may sound like a clear path, but they were more like walking a tightrope. I cannot emphasize how this childhood made me who I am today.

As a paramedic in Springfield there were several calls that challenged me more than others because they were either for my brother or one of his pals at the group home where he lived later on.

Summer 1990. Island Pond Road Group Home Run: cardiac arrest, my brother's friend. We get the radio call on State Street, city center, by the vocational school about three miles from my brother's group home. Cardiac arrest. I know it is either my brother or a friend, so I push on the accelerator and we fly there in minutes. I maintain my composure as I hustle our first-in equipment through the front door, my partner trailing behind. Staff members lead us right to my brother's room. *So, this is how it ends*, I think, *no, no*. One of the group home staff is doing CPR on a youngster on the floor just inside the door. At first, I can't see who the patient is. My heart skips a beat. But as I push into the room I can see it is not my brother but his friend. It isn't much of a relief because I know the boy as my brother's long-time friend, and he is like another brother to me.

We go through the protocol: taking care of the airway first and getting a quick look on the monitor. We establish an IV and push the meds with the rhythm of CPR. No sufficient response. He had died. Now, we are left with the process of going through the motions in hope of a miracle. I catch myself scanning the room as if sensing his ghost; his eyes, now fixated, stare out past me. I recall his bright, smiling eyes when I used to visit Doug. It hurts me to even look at him while working the code; this wasn't a peaceful passing after a long and well-lived life. My brother has been removed from the room, which I appreciate, but I keep seeing his saddened face in my mind. The group home staff is also distraught. They are as close and caring as a family.

Treating someone in this situation who has been close to you emotionally is unimaginably difficult, and the time moves even slower.

Over the years I had several emergency responses to my brother's group home. A few of those were for Doug and they were taxing on my nerves. I would remain cool; even my partners couldn't fathom the pain I felt. There is no place for drama in this profession. The job is to assess, treat, and transport. At least that's what I was trained to think.

These calls taught me a lot about life. They taught me that a patient is never just a patient—they are always someone's brother or sister. For that I learned to treat everyone like a brother or sister; even if I didn't like them, I treated them like a family member who was just, well, difficult.

But the more important thing I learned by treating such an amazing person whom I knew deeply and spiritually was *the need to treat a patient's spiritual injury or illness as I had to for my brother.* You see, in the back of the ambulance I couldn't simply go through the physical treatments for my brother without treating *him.* This was my only brother, whom I would give my last breath for and now needed my help. How could I treat him on a solely physical level?

12 August 1990. Island Pond Road Group Home Run: patient with seizures, Doug. It is a hot summers day when I get yet another call for my own brother. It is de-ja-vu receiving the same call as the recent cardiac arrest of my little brother's best friend. The memory sends chills up my spine. I can see that boy's face, his eyes, as I last saw it: dead, drained of life. I hit the gas, slide into the group home parking lot, and walk into the house the same way each time—forcing that image from my mind and confident death will not take my brother away, not today. I march in, never run, determined I can reverse any ailment by will and will alone. A quick assessment reveals the same torturous scenario I grew up with, and it infuriates me down deep, to the point my hands start tremoring. The same damned "spells" as Dr. Joe used to call them. Seizures with some neuro-pathophysiology doctors could not understand. How dare this return constantly making his life miserable. I ignore the bystanders as I hold my brothers arm and shoulder tightly, just like when we were kids.

"I'm here for you Doug, let's get you through this."

We carry my brother out to the idling Braun Ford ambulance. I love the sound of the growling diesel ambulance. It has that steady, persistent power that confirms it's alive and ready to carry your precious cargo to the hospital. At times like these you need *something* to depend on. My partner says she will put in an IV but can't find a vein as his are flat from dehydration. We find one in his shoulder, but it's not a great location. I find another on his dorsal foot, access that, and get some fluid flowing. My partner asks if we should administer valium for the seizure type activity.

"How about 8-10 mg?" she asks.

"He takes 60 plus milligrams a day, P.O." I say.

"Sixty milligrams a day?"

"Yes, what we have won't touch him, let's just get a move on."

I know this grand mal type seizure can rage on for hours, even days. There is some newer medicine that works at the hospital, so I can only hope to get him there safely.

As we bounce down the road, Doug clasps his hands and wrings them tightly as he would often do in obvious distress or pain. I wonder, was it like a crushing headache or just confusion he felt? I will never know. He is sweating profusely. The monitor displays a rapid heart rate; he is always pounding over 130. I think, *Why? What's causing all of this?*

"Just like back in the 1970's when I sat with you, Doug, nothing's changed, I still can't really help you."

He looks me straight in the eye as he always does, grimacing, clenched teeth grinding loudly, sweat soaked, pale, eyes wide with fear, pain, confusion.

"I'm sorry, Doug, I think I failed you, I'm so sorry... I'm really sorry." I whisper in his ear. I lean forward over the cot so the driver can't see in the rear view mirror or hear over the engine noise. "I just want you to be comfortable, live your life without all this pain. Do you understand what I'm saying?"

Douglas grunts, "Yeah," through clenched teeth. He begins to moan, muscles tensed to the density of stone, veins distended from his forehead, convulsing with sharp body spasms. What kind of creator allows this to happen to his creation? The question I would ask a thousand times beginning at a young age. This must be out of his control as it is mine.

Doug's eyes roll back, then to the left, and all I can do was hold on and pray, dig down deep. No medicine is going to cure this. I continue to pray and hold his arms so he can sense me there. Racing through the city, down East Columbus boulevard, we smash over potholes like a ship crashes over waves.

"God, please stop this," I say as I stare at nothing and pray to whom I could not see. I hear Doug groan in agreement, low and deep, almost a growl.

He quiets. I look down again, and he is staring at me, the spasms ceased, and he is serenely focused on me. It takes me by surprise. What just happened?

"Hey… hey," I call up to my partner. "Slow it down over the craters. We're doing OK." We ride into the hospital calmly and quietly. Doug just stares at me as if I have given him some relaxing miracle drug. I have given no valium, no medication whatsoever. Was it the fluid? Maybe it cooled his body temperature down, but that's reaching.

Sure, I can't say my prayers had anything to do with his miraculous recovery, but I can't say they did not. Prayers are for strength and guidance—my way of communicating that need—not for miracles. I told the ER doctor of the sudden change in seizure type activity to normal base level mentation, not a postictal, confused state that usually follows. I wasn't expecting a logical response. The doctor replied, "Sure, what other treatment could have such an effect?"

On reflection: am I really making a difference in Doug's life, and does my faith help? I believe it helped that I was consistently there for him during these painful episodes. Regarding faith, yes, I have seen our faith work powerfully in his life. A doctor once said Doug would be dead by the age of six; to that, we laughed when he outlived that mark three times over. It helped to have a good shepherd with him. It did not have to be me, but who else was going to be there in this capacity?

A prayer alone does not usually have direct, immediate, and physical results. To stop one of his spells would be to stop a lightning storm; and it had never changed that quickly: a sudden lull with calm. No medication did that for him. I have prayed intensely for days and weeks while he suffered with only temporary relief, otherwise nothing but agony. Why had relief come swiftly this time? We may never know. I understood from staff that when I was not there, nothing good happened. Maybe that is my perception, but that is what the staff said. Life does have its mystery with the power of good work versus the void left by nothing. Besides the best family, staff, and neurologists' he must have had access to a higher power. It takes perseverance to win these battles, but the war had just begun.

FISHERS OF PEOPLE IN NEED

Emergency Medical Services (EMS) can be either the most practical blue collar work or the most mysterious. It is a simple system under the umbrella of the 911 emergency call system, which is as random as a lottery. Anyone can dial those three numbers at any time for any reason, from a drunk to a train wreck or a mass shooting. The range of calls is almost indescribable. What is even more mysterious is when a stranger—out of hundreds of thousands of 911 calls— receives a medic who seems meant to be there for them. I've been at scenes where we've needed a foreign speaker and who should respond but that very person. Ask any medic who has done the job for years and they are sure to have some interesting calls that involve friends, family, or people they knew. It is even harder to explain in larger cities, like New York. I have responded to calls from immediate family, extended family friends, old high school buddies from out of town, friends, and family of friends. Sometimes the odds are overwhelming, and I wonder why I can't win the lottery. If there is one aspect that has kept me doing this crazy work for so long it is that opportunity to help people. Through time and experience you learn that you can relate to all people; we are not always so different. That is what much of this book is about.

However, I must be honest: I am not so liberal in response to those three numbers. Not all people need you or want help. I have had days where my partner and I were the only ambulance responding to dozens of people who truly did not need our help. They were taking advantage of the system. Some of these people were manipulative, destructive, and harmful to us as well as the community. I could see we must use resources wisely to help those in genuine need—like children and the vulnerable, who do not always get the resources and attention they need. That is a challenge in this new world. We are, to some extent, fishers of people in need.

26 October 2006. Small Town Massachusetts: schizophrenic episode. The ten-year-old stands on the side of the road with the state case worker waiting for us. I approach slowly and get down on one knee to be at her level. The dispatcher had noted the call was for a frightened young lady with schizophrenia. I do not have much experience with this illness in children, so it is challenging to gain her confidence. I am a father with a ten year old of my own, so I know to talk about all the things that make her happy and keep the mood light.

Once in the back of the ambulance, the girl begins talking with someone in a hallucination. I look to the case worker sitting on the back bench for guidance. I follow her lead, and coordinating an open and honest discussion with the patient *while acknowledging this is a hallucination* makes the ride a comfortable one for our young patient. At the hospital, she initially refuses to go inside. I tell her the hospital stories of my own two daughters and how they overcame their fears. The message is crystal clear, this is a good place to be. She stands a little taller and walks in with us to get the treatment she needs. No miraculous work on my part, but I like to think that my ability to relate to and comfort anyone in any situation is a service.

One might expect that we have no control over how many people we can help in a day; but we do have an option to fish about some. In my first decade, we had three ALS ambulances posted in the three ends of the city: north, south, east. When the city became busy, the dispatcher would send the last of these to center of the city. For the other two, it was a matter of completing their calls and paperwork to see who could hustle out the fastest for the next call.

It's been said there are two types of people: workers and bums. There is no doubt I was a worker. I wasn't perfect and certainly had my days, but by and large I was one of the fastest out and prided myself on it. Of course, there were other factors such as whether the next call would be the one with the greatest need. I had an understanding with my dispatchers, who needed their board cleared. A good dispatcher knows who is out there and who is going to get the work done, quickly, competently and without issue. For example, I could be dispatched to a basic call but then rerouted when something more urgent came in.

So, in rolling back out and making myself available, I was there for them. Even in the city center, I sometimes kept the truck rolling in circles, waiting, ready to go. It was this desire to do the job, this initiative, that allowed me to be there for the people who needed me. It pissed off many of my partners who wanted to hold back at the hospital, drink coffee, gossip or flirt with nurses (who clearly were not interested anyways).

I often asked dispatch if I could sit at a place called Five Mile Pond, off the main road through the city. It was close to our dispatch center and down the road from my home where I used to sit and watch the lights reflect off the pond. It wasn't the ocean, but it was all I had. I was comfortable there as I sipped my coffee. From this post I could get anywhere quickly. I would write notes from that day's calls and wonder what the hell I was doing with my life.

18:00. 25 August 1989. I respond to a small stone synagogue on the south edge of the city. The 911 call was for a 76-year-old man with chest pain. We walk up the massive stone steps and through the impressive arched wooden door to find our patient sitting on a bench, sweating and in some discomfort. He shoots me a look that says I do not belong there, get lost.

"Who called you guys? I don't need you, I'm fine. I know myself better than you, just leave me alone," he says, waving me off.

"Okay, I'll leave but for your friends outside who really care for you, could I just go through the motions, for them?"

The old timer looks at me with disgust like at a lost kid who stumbled into his Temple and didn't know shit. He was certainly right there.

I place my trusty cardiac monitor leads on him, knowing I'm not going to learn anything exceptional, and take his vitals. They're perfect. I am concerned with the profuse sweating, but he says he had taken his nitro tablets. He says the pain has subsided and refuses transport. He looks better already.

"This is a very impressive synagogue," I say, trying to establish more friendly footing. "I've always been impressed at the Jewish adherence to tradition. It takes a lot to stick to traditions these days."

He finally smiles and tells me, "This is the beginning of Sabbath (Shabbat). It begins Friday evening sunset and ends sunset Saturday."

I have always considered and respected other religions, knowing that if I had been born to a family that practiced Judaism or Islam or any other religion, then that might be what I would be practicing. Given I was a worldly twenty five years of age, I didn't know much at all about other religions. So, I asked questions. I learned through friends that the strong traditions and cultures of the Jewish handle suffering and death differently from Christians. The observant Jewish make decisions such as lifesaving procedures with the assistance of their Rabbi, physician, and referencing centuries of Jewish laws and oral traditions (Halacha). It all depends on their practice and situation.

Most of us are aware that Judaism is the monotheistic religion of the ancient Hebrews. Their religious traditions contrast with other religions regarding suffering and end of life. For those unfamiliar, you can refer to a brief definition of Judaism in the bibliography at the end of this book. I can tell you from experience, the more I understood of other cultures and religions, the better I could help those in times of need.

SPIRITUALITY AND RELIGION

I've thought, at all hours, over the past thirty-four years and counting on this subject. *Do spirituality and religion matter in the struggle between life and death—in suffering and in the last minute battle for your life? In what ways?* How and why as the sole person on scene can one help? We should all seek to answer these questions as we may face it sooner than we expect. What does that have to do with the job of a paramedic?

I am referring to those moments that a medic sees more than most and has the opportunity to help more than any other.

My mentor and the Medical Control Physician for most of my career once said to me that we (healthcare practitioners) *take care of people at the worst time of their life and therefore have an obligation to the patient.* I speculate that includes an obligation to listen, learn, and act on what the patient needs in those final moments. If you think that means pushing medication, a breathing tube, and off to the coroner, then maybe our system is somewhat broken. The scope of our state and national protocols is our first priority: to assess and follow the protocol, "save" the patient if we can. But what does that accomplish for patients that do not need saving, and is that all the patient needs or wants at that moment?

Some patients choose a "Comfort Care" Do Not Resuscitate (DNR) order depending on their condition. I will revisit the importance of that patient request and physician written order later, but the point here is that our obligation includes different demands in different patient situations. I speculate that for most patients the physical aspect at that stage of their life is *not* what's most important. Certainly, most everyone wants to be comfortable—not writhing in pain and discomfort in their last days, hours, and moments. And as medics we can do a good job of making them physically comfortable when orders are clear and complete. Some patients have prepared for their spiritual or holistic support, but that must work hand in hand with palliative care at home, which is a growing trend. Getting patients home from the hospital with end-of-life care can be a challenge and needs to be planned as carefully as possible. Ongoing skilled nursing care at home has always been another problem that continues until this day. Home care has improved; *however, our healthcare system and EMS have not fully recognized the need for this in the field.*

24 July 2011. Springfield. At the hospital two brothers, stand in the doorway talking with the discharging physician and case manager. Their tired, intense expressions show concern and contemplation. I stand by as they finish their conversation, and the doctor asks to talk with me to the side. I have a report from the patient's nurse and an envelope of patient paperwork, including a signed Do Not Resuscitate (DNR)/Comfort Care Order. The doctor informs me that the patient's sons asked to rescind the DNR just as we are prepared to transport the father home to die. This creates a problem, and a decision must be made. He explains their change of heart based on their religious beliefs in these familiar words.

"At first, they understood 'comfort care' as supporting him to get him home—oxygen, fluids, pain medications, positioning, no CPR, no advanced procedures, medicines, etc. which is true as the form has these options. Now the patient's condition had quickly worsened, and he may not make the entire ride home, so I can check the box for ACLS procedures en route (which changes the order to 'resuscitate.') Once they understood that it would include more medicines and lifesaving measures meant to prolong his life such as CPR (and possibly a return to the hospital) the family changed their decision because his wishes were to die a natural death."

The doctor further explains that according to the sons' interpretation of Islamic law, they had told him, "When death is inevitable, the person should be allowed to die without these unnecessary procedures."

So that creates a new problem that requires a decision. When the patient cannot survive the trip home without advanced procedures then the "natural death" chosen *should happen where they are*. In this case, that means staying at the hospital. Transport is very risky. If the patient passes away on the road home, then we must return his body to the hospital. That is because an ambulance cannot legally transport a "dead body" to a private home in our state.

In this case, the patient does not have much time left he and his family must make a decision based on this question: Do you want him to remain comfortable and die in his hospital room, or do you want us to try to transport him "quickly" home, hoping he makes it all the way?

We contact our Medical Control Physician and advise that the sending physician changed the Comfort Care order to full DNR under the family's guidance. We transported him home swiftly. He was made comfortable in his room surrounded by family at home. This time we were fortunate. We ask that physicians understand this in advance and work with family to make these decisions sooner when possible so no one is placed in this predicament.

On this case we are also working with a family whose religion I am not that familiar with. It is not as if classes are offered to medics to learn more about who we are trying to help in our city. In order to work as a team I have to do my own research to try to learn more about their faith each time. Clearly, religion matters to this patient and his family at those last moments between life and death.

Islam is the second largest religion in the world with 1.8 billion followers. The numbers where I worked were small but present and growing. The monotheistic religion of the Muslims teaches that there is only one God and that the prophet Muhammed is the messenger of God (Allah). Islamic law is not Sharia law. I have been told Sharia is closer to their holy books' divine and philosophical guidance; this includes the precepts of Islam, the Quran (the central religious text of Islam), and the Hadith (a record of words, actions, and silent approvals by the Prophet Muhammad). It has been my experience that Muslim traditions can be complicated regarding end-of-life situations; but family will usually guide the process. This is because many diverse traditions are accepted due to social, demographic, denominational, and cultural variations in practice. As with all faiths in this situation, communication has been the key.

Medics are "there for the patient" at these times and can be of great assistance to the patient and family. Sometimes we must be there when even family and friends are not because suffering and death are too painful to watch. At times those closest fade away. In my experience, the physician and religious leaders are often not present either as they cannot be everywhere for everyone. Paramedics are strategically posted in disparate areas and thus can be the only people responsible, accountable, and most importantly "there for them" in time.

Urban, suburban, and rural EMS systems have always operated differently in expanded roles to ensure patients get the services they need. Some suburban and rural areas depend more on police officers or volunteer squads who are EMTs because resources are limited. In some urban systems, there are senior paramedics who have been trained to understand all aspects of care and act as patient advocates to access resources such as: a visiting nurse, palliative care professionals, psychiatric care, or even assistance programs like meals-on-wheels. Some of these are accessed through local resources like town hall, senior centers, volunteer groups, or local religious organizations.

In the summer of 1992, we had a woman well known to us who called 911 daily. She was an older woman of European decent. She had a heavy accent, and her dress and shoes appeared to be from centuries past. Some made fun of her antics, which included drinking liquor and calling us daily (a regular) to find her in a game of hide and seek at her house. She would run around the neighborhood throwing items at whoever attempted to help. I had been there several times and worked a truck with my partner, Laurie, who was received well by the elderly woman—in part because her kindness and insistence to help never wavered. Laurie had just checked the kitchen and joined the patient and I in the living room of the small, dilapidated house. Our conversation went something like this.

"Alyona, let us help you. I see there's no food in your cabinets or your refrigerator. What are you eating?" asked Laurie.

"Oh, not much, the oats. I drink water."

"That's not enough to keep you healthy. We need to have more meals delivered, but you need to answer the door and accept them. Can you do that?"

"No, I'm busy. Leave me," Alyona grumbled.

The police officer on scene added, "Alyona, you must accept the food that's been delivered. The volunteers have said you're not answering your door when they come." He went to check that her doorbell and phone were working.

"How do you feel? Do you get tired, weak, hungry? Laurie continued.

"Yes, hungry, tired."

"That may be because you're not getting enough good food. We discussed your medication delivery a couple days ago. Where are your new ones?"

"I don't know."

"We need to get you some more help."

"Is there anyone at your church who can help you?" I asked, noting all the church announcements strewn across the dining table along with pictures of saints, the only art on the drab aqua green walls.

"No, I don't see them… I can't get a ride to the church," she mumbled, tearing up.

"OK, well, maybe we can call them and look into that."

"My phone doesn't work." She shook her head.

"Okay, we'll call for you."

I continued to try to get answers in the back of the ambulance.

"Did you eat the food that was delivered?"

"I miss the women at church," Alyona responded.

"Did you ever get your medicines?" I asked.

"I miss my friends at the church. Can we go there now?"

Clearly, her church life and friends were more important than food or medicine to her. We transported Alyona to the hospital like so many other "regulars" and discussed her situation with staff. Her request to connect with her church could be confused with a need for "socialization" for which she could be referred to a local senior center. I made it clear what she wanted as she was very specific.

Being attentive and on scene is key. It doesn't matter who or what agency is in that role to garner the needed services as long as it's done. This is especially important when the patients are not transported or don't have family or friends to advocate for them. By communicating these concerns better and sharing our patient care reports (PCR's) the larger system can be more effective.

In the 1980's and 90's in our system, medical control physicians served multiple functions and were unable to work in the field. Today, there is growing involvement from a field-oriented physicians. Palliative care and community paramedicine have been effective in some areas of America and the rest of the world. With hospitals crowded or short-staffed and funding for such "specialty care" cut, we need more than ever to evolve and grow in this area.

Considering all this you would think the medical community would fully understand patients' needs at home, but I usually found that was not the case. Not all patients go to a facility or alert family, friends, or even their doctor (if they have these) for all their care, as my experiences here depict. Therefore, all aspects of patient care must be considered when we arrive on scene for unrelated complaints. A paramedic's job has always been an intersection of health care, public health, and public safety. Health care includes the recognition of definitive care aspects such as general health, psychiatric and social services. But we also recognize a wide range of patient needs for services such as food, clothing, shelter, counseling, long term treatments for illnesses and injuries, and home care assistance. Of course, palliative or hospice care may or may not be in place; if not, sometimes we need to transport patients to the hospital so the physicians can assess the need and resources for those services at that time. Even if services are in place, sometimes patients are not cooperative or resist assistance.

In recent years, discussions in EMS circles led to the decision to support patients psychologically in emergencies and simple transports, and as a result, training and protocols improved. This need first came to light with patients suffering from psychiatric illnesses and in crisis with limited resources. The need for expanding the scope of psychiatric field care was apparent because in such cases you cannot treat someone without addressing the underlying problem.

One difference between a psychiatric crisis and other illnesses is if you could not manage the patient, then you couldn't transport them safely. The problem had to be corrected without question, and that need advanced pre-hospital care. Medics are not trained psychiatrists but basic recognition, understanding, and treatment could be learned and practiced. Unfortunately, these protocols were at first limited by mainstream health care organizations, who did not wish to acknowledge pre-hospital EMS as *additional* providers with actual treatments. That improved in part for psychiatric care out of necessity and demonstrable success achieved for patients.

Our main job is physical: a blue-collar move-the-patient in the UPS-style truck driver job. Play medic and treat them per the scientific, evidence-based protocols as a pre-programmed delivery guy. That's a medic some say—a delivery guy, a low-skilled driver—and at certain times that's all you need, two lifters to move the patients to care. But the obvious fact that every white-collar physician, priest, minister and rabbi wants to ignore is that *medics have more access to those most spiritual, self-assessing last moments of life than they do.* That access is *everything* to that person at that time.

In other words, how effective is a physician who only sees you once a year or a priest who sees you for an hour on Sunday at assessing and guiding your physical and spiritual well-being? Who is there at the hour of our death at 3:00am?

I once produced a photo-journal on EMTs working at these critical times, times of suffering, illness, death. For my photography course I rode third and recorded situations while working full-time. I shot roles of black and white film discretely recording patient and medic interactions. A few of these captured the quick but significant bond between patient and caring medic at the worst time.

In one photo, a crew is performing CPR on a patient while he is wheeled on a gurney from his home. If you look closely, standing back against the house by the driveway is a priest; at the time, I was unaware he was even there. I did not see him until I developed the photograph. He must have been called to the house. It was a commendable but rare sighting. Attendance and customary rituals by religious leaders should be more prevalent in our society because you can't schedule these moments in a church or place of worship. As experienced practitioners we know there are good and bad deaths regardless of who is there or what they do. As you read about my experiences in this book, I try to grasp the non-physical and spiritual suffering that takes place every day and what I did or could not do to help alleviate it.

To remedy this suffering is not possible without understanding patients and their beliefs, culture, and traditions. There are several prominent organized religions in my multi-cultural area to consider: Christianity, Judaism, Islam, Hinduism, Buddhism. While not organized religions, we also provide comfort and care for *everyone*—the agnostic spiritualist and even the atheist, some of whom rethink their spirituality during suffering or the last moments of life. Whatever the faith, many cultures embrace the end-of-life with respect and even ritual or ceremony.

By the late 1990's, it appeared to me that some families had devolved away from receiving the faith-oriented end-of-life services or spiritual support at home. I don't have any hard data on this observation any more than I do of the closing churches or shrinking congregations in our area. I just saw it less often on my calls. And I am not sure this was due to patient choice or simply because those services were no longer arranged by family as in years past. I recall seeing these services, especially in the older neighborhoods in the 1980's. Later on, into the 2000's, they were more often only seen in facilities such as nursing homes. Over my career, I have observed more people choosing to die in the tranquility, privacy, and peace of their own home. There are aspects of that choice that can be planned and mobilized.

Outpatient palliative care is a plan of care providing a holistic approach; it supports the patient's religious, spiritual, physical, and socio-psychological needs at home. Now, when you hear "holistic" you might imagine hippies dancing about in tie-dye smocks smoking grass, but that's not what I'm referring to. You might imagine a priest anointing patients with oil and incensing with smoke from a medieval thurible swinging on chains to religious chants. That's great if that's what the patient's beliefs call for. However, I'm simply talking about offering complete care. For our part as EMS, think of it as a supportive conversation with our patient while assessing their needs for this real end-of-life situation. The patient and their support team can do as they wish in the amount of time they have. Some patients will have their plan and people in place; others may need last minute assistance. In my experience many patients will be alone and therefore need our assistance. Then there is just the decision whether to transport or not.

Providing spiritual care along with the physical by EMS requires a continuum of the good work provided at the patient's home, so communication and collaboration are key. I am not suggesting we medics become palliative care specialists, just that we begin to understand and mobilize useful concepts and resources, which is already what we do to a point. Look at some of the principles of palliative care we already provide:

1. Affirm life and recognize dying as a normal process in which the patient needs support.

2. Respect the patient's desire to neither hasten nor prolong death according to their beliefs.

3. Relieve pain and distress.

4. Integrate psychological and psychosocial care.

5. Involve family and patient as a whole.

6. Provide Medical Comfort Care, Do Not Resuscitate (DNR) orders with specific orders (ventilation and transport to hospital) signed by the clinician, patient, or patient's representative.

The last principle missing from our treatment is the *spiritual support or religious support access.*

This would be the actual religious, spiritual, or cultural process/ceremony desired by that patient with their chosen faith. All we as medics need to do is be patient and allow time for such practices when possible. I'm not suggesting medics become spiritual or religious experts; rather, that we recognize the need for such treatment and assist as we can. As a group in a profession, do we have that capability, or *is that spirit even in us* to provide? My guess is "each according to his ability."

Faith as a Treatment

Medics and providers might consider that in providing spiritual support in various ways or religious services we are providing *emergency* health care. Physical suffering is only one aspect of the dying process. Understanding the root cause of non-physical suffering and how to relieve that pain can and should be part of our patient treatment. Just as we now proactively treat our patients with psychological distress and suffering so too can we help patients with this perplexing end-of-life suffering in those moments. .

It's an emergency because we all know it can't wait if the patient is dying, and increased distress has proven to contribute to and even hasten death. Most of the faithful desire a peaceful end-of-life process supported by their choice of ritual, ceremony, or tradition. To treat non-physical suffering, we must understand the patients' beliefs and a little of their cultural influences. It is not in the scope of this writing to define in detail all aspects of all religions, but I try to note the pertinent faith or spirituality as I recall my experiences.

Hospice and a Good Death at Home

On the practical side, on some hospice cases, why would the patient planning to die at home not just stay at home? Why would they need to call or request an ambulance? At times patients' need arising medical problems to be assessed for treatment by a physician representative, tests, or emergency treatment for comfort. Then there are all the patients who are not on hospice and no one can predict when the end will come along with those same needs. Sometimes when medics arrive at a patient's home in this situation, the patient changes their mind and requests to stay at home; these decisions change constantly for some.

Clinically, *almost everything we are taught* to do is for the physical aspect of patient care, and the end-of–life moment is treated as a separate protocol for which we provide comfort care and then the "termination of efforts." This is when many medics just disconnect, pack up their gear, and get back in service. I found today many practitioners (in all fields) avoid conversations of comfort care, DNR paperwork, and spirituality and end-of-life plans with their patients—at least that's what patients and families tell me at 3 am when grandpa is dying in his bedroom. This, ironically, is also the time when grandpa wants to talk about his religious beliefs so he can "come to terms" and die peacefully.

So maybe our treatments should be what the patient wants at that time and not what the doctor dictated two months ago during a five minute appointment. Who says the all-knowing health care establishment are always right about *their* perspective of end-of-life care anyway? Is that what you have experienced? No offense, some practitioners are outstanding, but overall, everyone must agree this system needs improvement.

One priority is to know are we resuscitating him physically or not? The answer is not always apparent. Where is a written, dated, and signed DNR that we can withhold cardio-pulmonary resuscitation? We search the refrigerator door (traditional place to post), kitchen drawers, etc. Talking with the family, who is typically the patient's vocal advocate as he is passing, is like talking to several more patients who all need our support. They don't need medicinal solutions like sedatives suggested by the big pharma companies; rather, a compassionate, supportive, even holistic care (spirit, mind, and body) approach.

What could all this look like on scene to an untrained observer?

23:30. 10 November 1987. We are called to assist an elderly patient with difficulty breathing a in two-story house downtown. We get delayed on another scene and arrive about twenty minutes after the first medic on scene. We haul our gear up to the second floor apartment.

"What's with the patient?" my medic partner asks.

"He's dead. DNR. Didn't want us. Wanted his pastor or someone."

"Did you call anyone?"

"I tried this number he had on a small note pad but no answer."

The old man is in a fetal position on the bed, hands clasped as if still in prayer. He looks peaceful.

"What did you do?"

"I called med con, tried to make him comfortable, but he wasn't cooperating. We couldn't really do much, so we just…"

"So, you just what, watched him die?"

We later learned that the medic did try to comfort the old man as best he knew how, but clearly he didn't do enough to get the resource needed (a pastor) there. A person's spirituality or relationship with God is a private matter, which they may guard at moments such as "at the hour of our death." At that hour, medics are usually not the last person one wants to see; therefore we can be more attentive to who and what each patient desires. We either need to get a pastor (on call) there or have some training to assist the patient at that time.

So how is it that performing this stupid job can a simpleton realistically figure out what matters to a soul in those final moments, objectively and subjectively? The answer is simple: observation. Of the four types of observational researchers, I have been a "Complete Participant." Like any controlled research study, the method is to immerse yourself in the situation with your subjects and repeatedly and closely observe what happens second to second and record it. Did I take notes? I've made thousands on paper and in my head, unforgettable to the smallest detail. So why didn't I become a scholar in all of this? I would have studied more theories, read more books, and became a peer-reviewed authority, but *there is no substitute for first-hand experience*. My only expertise is in real situations with real people and results. A medic is a realist.

The recent evolution in beliefs from the medical authorities *suggest that science has replaced religion or even spirituality in patient care today*. Just read any medical journal today. I've witnessed a desire among patients, especially the elderly and terminally ill, for the return of religion because of the failures they experienced of cold, unfeeling science and technology. Authorities snidely claim that spirituality hasn't made a discovery in thousands of years. Another common academic retort is unseen forces that don't exist cannot cure or heal the ailments of human existence.

So, I ask, has science and its medications saved us? From what I have witnessed first-hand on a daily basis, it doesn't appear that the scientific solution works alone nor was it conceived as a sole solution. In fact, there are *millions*, a measurable quantity, of cases of physical and mental suffering today that attest to the failure of the science. Take, for example, anti-depressants. Suicide is an increasing leading cause of death in some age groups (1999-2016 CDC), despite more pharmaceuticals being prescribed in response. At the time of writing this, there are 140 deaths per day by suicide. This all goes to show that pharmaceuticals alone are not a panacea for such complex diseases and disorders. I've seen it, worked it, studied it, *lived it* as kids to elders died in front of me.

In fact, you name the ailment and one of the 4,000 plus FDA approved medication treatments and we've *all* seen the failures. Science alone is not the answer, and our health care system is not the most successful in the world. It is broken, and I think getting worse by the year. Recall one of my questions: can the medical community's faith in science/technology work together with a faith in spirituality/religion? I think it better because alone it is looking very ugly.

Technology has become an excuse for sheer lack of empathy in all aspects of care. The computer self-check-in Kiosk Triage Nurse (an ATM-like box) in some Emergency Room lobbies today is a good example of that. With no triage nurse present, signage directs you or maybe a security guard at the kiosk. If you have not had the experience, this is simply a screen with graphic icons on a floor stand where you enter your general information, insurance card, chief complaint, and symptoms on a touch screen. That data goes to a screen in the ER where the staff can see it and respond when they have the time or if the complaint is a priority. Some hospitals claim great success and reduced wait times of up to fifteen minutes. However, the lack of an experienced and empathetic triage nurse can make this experience as isolated and frustrating as a dysfunctional fast food drive through. Is this reassuring for the elderly who are not so technically inclined? There are many shortfalls when applying industrial dynamics to health care, and I'm not alone in my concerns. Should we treat patients like products on a factory's assembly line floor?

Of course, there are some commendable, pioneering clinicians using a multi-therapeutic approach and listening to their patients with success. They are the minority, but they are also a reason for hope.

We medics are often witnesses to the most difficult moments in life; we're posted down the street to be there first. In my first twenty years on the job, I never thought I would write a book on this aspect of my work. I learned from what I've witnessed; spirituality as practiced by people of every faith is one facet that truly vitalizes our life while we live it and dignifies our death as we face it. Our spirituality emanates from our soul but is often ignored in our "practical" culture, even at our most vulnerable times: illness and death. Naturally, all religions emphasize spiritualism as an essential element of their faith. A person can be spiritual without organized religion, but not religious without spirit. Spirituality and the sense of your soul as a common denominator can unite people of different religions.

As care providers we can help patients more by understanding and respecting these concepts. That can be a challenge in these times when fewer Americans are affiliated with an organized religion. A Pew research study (2007- 2014) found a decrease in religious beliefs by a growing minority, called "nones," for no affiliation, mostly of the millennial generation, who say they do not belong to any organized religion. These "nones" now account for

23% of the adult population, up from 16% in 2007. * Overall, the Religious Landscape Study found that America's religious numbers are better than most industrialized countries, but the decrease in those who "consider religion to be important" in this field would need to be convinced in the value of helping those who do.

8 October 2004. It is a typical hospice ride home for this 72-year-old gentleman, a ride that is becoming more and more common. Increasingly, people seem to be making the choice to die in peace and dignity in their own home. The patient is exhausted from his cancer and subsequent stress: physically, emotionally, and spiritually. As usual the hospital discharge procedures have delayed his transport, and now they are concerned if he will even make it home.

It always amazes me how hospital staff cut these discharges so close when it is so important to the patient to be at home when they die, not in the hospital or an ambulance. Assessing him in his room wasn't confidence building; he was asleep, pale, unresponsive to voice, with degenerating vitals. Once we load him into the truck, he comes to life. He talks on the way home, and I listen. It is mostly about returning to his house to be with family. A few rural towns over, we arrive at his house surrounded by fields. His family is waiting. He says he wants to see them but is afraid of dying in front of them or saying the wrong thing—the medications he's on can muddle his thoughts. Seeing he was a man of faith, I tell him that while his worries are reasonable, he only need talk to one person and the others will be honored and happy he is home. He says he is "not home yet but will be soon." We arrive and quickly carry him in. With some assistance, we get him to his back porch where he can look out at the vast country fields. He acknowledges his family, looks up at the sun, and closes his eyes once again.

Spiritual: A universal human state of mind, sacred or transcendent, to both religious and non-religious people. For the purposes of this book, this usually means a personal relationship with God or a higher power. It can be an individual's journey to find a truth that they have not found in organized religion. There is a significant number of people who hold a diverse set of personal beliefs regarding their soul, God, life, death, nature, and everlasting life.

I speculate that some spiritualists who are not religious may have been involved in an organized religion but left partially or completely because of conflicts with particular agendas and practices, especially unethical ones. In the communities I served as a medic, I believe some were agnostic—perhaps as much as a quarter of the demographic we served.

I know some devoutly religious adherents dismiss the authenticity of this group, but I contend at the end-of-life they deserve to have their beliefs recognized as any other. I have witnessed hundreds of people struggle in the final hour with their religious identity and beliefs, and I think they should have access to assistance just like those who observe organized religions. For example: a parishioner who may have been psychologically or physically abused by a church member or knows someone who was a victim of abuse, fraud, or misguidance and thus left their church. Some of these people may still be very spiritual or religious in their heart. The may even practice in their own way, but they left the services of their church. When approaching the end-of-life, a patient should have access to a network that can direct them to services that will guide them in these difficult times and a pastor.

As for the religious who have not adhered to their religion for various reasons, they may choose to have a friend or family read prayers at their home when very ill or at the end-of-life. In the Bible you are instructed to build and worship the Lord at your altar and keep God within your heart— not a church building. As far as I know of the Bible, God nor Jesus never stated it was a requirement that you commit your life or loyalty to a priest, congregation of people, or a building: *only to God.*

WE ARE SOULS

We are souls with bodies, not bodies with souls. That is one of the most important things I learned as a child and repeatedly as a medic. Many of us hear this lesson but do not listen and learn. When your job is to go from crisis to crisis, day in and day out around the clock, it can make you stoic, methodical, cold, callous; it helps to get the job done without becoming emotionally attached. To compartmentalize. It's a form of self-protection, and in that mode you can be very detached and objective. Some learn to listen and observe more than what the job requires, think deeper, and, conversely and ironically, become emotionally involved. Those who knew me when I worked hundreds of hours on the street thought I was as emotionally detached and distant as humanly possible. Actually, the opposite was true.

When you observe person after person suffer, come close to death, or slowly die, you do see an aspect of humanity that is otherwise invisible—or rather, intentionally ignored. At times, when I think of all the suffering and death that I've witnessed, I cannot help but get a little watery-eyed; not because I'm a bleeding heart, but because life to death is such a lonely trip. Remember, we're all leaving, so shouldn't we all be prepared? Most are not. In my observations, not all of us are as spiritual and soulful as we thought when the time comes. I've seen hundreds live those last moments distraught, confused, lost, alone, believing they haven't completed their journey, uncertain, faithless, confounded; despite me or a loved-one doing our best to provide consolation. Is that not a greater emergency than the inability to provide physical remedies? Will we wake up some day and regret this history as a community, a culture, and a nation?

Now, for those truly, deeply spiritual, soulful, and religious people I have observed it is often different. Certainly not a guarantee to a peaceful passing—I've seen innocent and righteous people suffer and die horrible deaths, too. The numbers don't matter. What does matter is that so often I would see someone who had suffered but kept their faith those last moments, and it seemed to make their passing with peace and confidence. That is not sad and can even be inspirational. These folks aren't necessarily clutching a Bible or other scripture, reciting a prayer, or conducting a spiritual ritual at their time of death. But people reach out beyond themselves in various ways: with words, gestures, symbols, poetry, music, or their last works. Some pray silently, communicating with their God or observe a moment of silence. This silence is always filled with spirit, hope, and values.

7 September 1987. My partner, Jake, and I receive a call for respiratory distress in the south end—little Italy. We enter the old, two-family tenement on the ground floor through the unlocked door, calling out for someone at home. We follow hardwood floors through immaculate rooms with white linen curtains and come to a small back room that appears to be an *altar room*. A sprawling, ornate Romanesque-style carpet guides our eyes to the small, white linen-covered home altar table against the back wall, complete with candles, a cross, and picture of Jesus on the wall with statues.

Kneeling in front of the table is an elderly gentleman dressed in a suit and praying with his head bowed. We pause and quietly approach.

"Sir. Sir, excuse me?" Jake says. "Sir, you called for an ambulance? What can we help you with?"

The gentleman does not respond but continues to pray. We can hear his lungs rattle and see him having trouble breathing in the classic Cheyne–Stokes pattern, faster and deeper. Jake quickly grows impatient with what he sees as a ritualistic waste of time. He approaches, gently and respectfully, and asks to listen to the man's lungs with his scope through the thin suit jacket.

"Sir. Sir, with all due respect I need to listen to your lungs."

As he puts the scope against the suit jacket, the man raises his right hand as if to say "stop." Jake keeps the scope on his back and the man twists sharply, again raising his hand.

"Can we just give him a minute?" I ask.

Jake turns to me with a pinpricked look.

"It's OK, let him pray. It's important to him," I say.

Jake walks back, leans towards me, and says, "Don't you think he needs some medicine?" Always the medicine. I am not yet a medic, so it is an often repeated reminder that apparently I need from the all-knowing and terminally frustrated Jake.

"Sure, but this moment here is sacred to him. It's his medicine, and this patient can't be rushed," I say in a hushed tone, though the patient can probably hear. He had probably been in congestive heart failure for a week or more, so, as the ER docs always said, what's a few minutes?

The gentleman arises a few minutes later and is very polite and cooperative, his easy demeanor reminding me of my Italian-born grandfather, Albert. We treat the gentleman on scene, and on the bus he perks up a little with the oxygen.

As we wheel him into a drab curtained patient room, he again clasps his hands, head bowed, silent, soulful, maybe in prayer. The nurse hustles in and thrusts her face in his.

"Sir. Sir, you awake? Excuse me for interrupting, but there's a lot we have to do here. Sir," the irked nurse repeats in frustration.

"Christ, can you give him a little space, respect?" I ask.

I understand that we have our job to do and if not done quickly, then the doctor is not going to be satisfied. That's one problem. Everything must always be quicker, more intelligent, more powerful. But I wrote down a question in my notes, "What really got the old gentleman here, as in this far in life?" He was 97 years old and on very few medications. I doubt any of us will be in as good of shape as he is at that age—and spiritually, soulfully, faithfully? We healthcare providers were all proud of ourselves for the quick forty-five minutes we spent working on him, but how far did we get? It was not modern science and medications that kept this man physically and spiritually alive. They have no patience or deeper understanding of our existence.

Psalm 37:7, "Be still before the Lord and wait patiently for him."

8 July 1989. We are on hour thirteen of a twenty-four hour shift, my third this week. Sipping black coffee with vitamins and trying to make sense of our second DOA of the day. Thus far we've had roughly a patient an hour with routine maladies otherwise. My partner, Walt I will call him, likes to make comments throughout the day. They range from observant to critical to sarcastic to flippant. These are usually targeted at me, but anyone is fair game. He likes to call me "Al" short for Albert, my middle name. We use these names as a form of anonymity from the crazy patrons and as a form of entertainment for ourselves. He's a smart and friendly and could be helpful if he wanted to be, but that would be too easy.

"So, you want to go get some ice cream, maybe have a coffee with the mayor?" he asks, and I completely ignore him because there is no correct answer.

I am trying to understand why those two patients (separate runs) just died alone at home and never called 911. Most medics could not care less because our job is only to save those who can be saved. Both patients were found sitting slumped in chairs as if waiting around for their moment to go. In both cases, the neighbors suspected something and called 911, but it was far too late to try to revive them. If we were there would that 'hour of our death' for them been more comfortable, insightful, religious, dignified?

Did they have families they could call? Did they live their lives and choose to die alone? Were they not religious, spiritual, or have someone who could be with them in those last moments of life? Did they know the end was coming and not plan for it, was that even possible? Or did they choose to die alone, maybe with their God, their memories of times and people past, or were they totally alone? I found some of these scenario's profoundly sad.

Walt and I had had similar conversations before. He senses I am thinking about this and nods his head in agreement, smiling, without even asking a question.

28 June 1990. A stone Roman Catholic Church of God. Sunday morning. A call comes in for an 83-year-old woman found unresponsive in her pew, possibly deceased.

She is attended to by the congregation and the pastor before we arrive. The patient appears to have passed some time before and had been sitting alone in the pew for a few hours. I estimate time of death at least 20-30 minutes earlier by the signs I can see. She is surrounded by some the congregation, most with their heads bowed and hands clasped. Many look as if they have been here for a century. We approach with more sensitivity than usual, probably because of the atypical environment. The priest speaks in soft tones; he is not overwhelmed as he has attended many in their dying moments and in death. Occasionally, he looks up at the grand ceiling as he if knows she is no longer in the pew. I find I am looking up myself—have to—I don't want to miss seeing the patient's spirit after all. I think he is performing the last rites but may have been too late. I'm not certain. He doesn't need our assessment, heart monitor, or technological gadgets to show him the obvious.

Now at this moment it's our job to work quickly, assess, start CPR, throw on the monitor, and treat aggressively. But this is considered a gray area because of the time passed, absence of signs of life, fixed pupils, and the steady, flat green line on my monitor. As I assess and try to find a pulse, I find her hands entwined with rosary beads. I can't help but notice the three Hail Mary beads between her thumb and fingers, cross dangling. They are wrapped tightly in her clutch. I don't want to remove them and pause to think, *Couldn't I leave these on? Shouldn't I leave these on? Are they not sacred?* We gently move her to the gurney first. I want to pronounce her with respect and hold off on the mechanical CPR clown show. But she has no significant signs, such as rigor of the jaw or extremities as of yet that I could make the call of Dead on Scene (DOS). No DNR was found in her pocketbook. Still, every move we make is respectful, steady, fluid, and mostly out of sight of the bystanders. Like a magician, I can complete every skill and task as I block my motions with body and work quickly with my hands.

It may be my perception, but my partner senses it too (and this EMT is about as sensitive as a block of wood). The death on this scene seems to have been natural and without the distress of most. The atmosphere is serene, with sunlight streaming in through stained glass windows. Even my thoughtless partner agrees that it is unfortunate that more people couldn't pass away in their house of God.

My thoughts on this scene lingered for days, weeks, months. I think of it to this very day. The day after, I had noted, "It is it is very unfortunate that our medical control physician and protocols (of the time) are so disconnected to the reality of the scene." Determining death on scene may appear simple, but it is a challenge for EMS and all faiths globally. It is a clinical process to determine "irreversible cessation of circulatory and respiratory functions and all functions of the entire brain including the brain stem." Unfortunately there is not a more advanced process, which would have allowed time for after death prayers (the Last Rites ritual and Anointing of the Sick is meant to take place *before* death), or for people to respectfully grieve in peace. Clearly, the patient had died, and her body in most religions is seen as sacred, to be left alone. In Christianity all seem in acceptance with moving the body as nothing after death is going to affect the soul's acceptance from God.

In EMS, ours is a black and white world in which this patient may not have had enough of a lead time with signs of death that we could determine death on scene and leave the body for the funeral home to take. This would have been beneficial for those on scene to have a peaceful closure, without the stress and confusion of medical intervention. We were and in some systems still are, obligated to perform CPR and transport. The latest protocol would have allowed us to cease resuscitation but only after twenty minutes of resuscitation if she remained asystolic (without a heart rhythm.) I noted, "Do our actions affect the resurrection of the dead for an everlasting communion with God?" I don't know. Is that death considered a good death, in that the patient was perhaps where she wanted to rest in peace at the hour of her death?

The friends and any family on such a scene who are clearly religious and for whom spiritual awareness is important are, from a community health perspective, potentially patients. These folks may be experiencing physical suffering or non-physical suffering themselves, and in my opinion could have benefitted more from our attention than the dead. Herein lies those problems on scene that are often overlooked. We're busy working a non-viable code, upsetting and confusing people, while elderly friends there may need medical attention. Each religion and cultural group have different expectations for such scenarios. To some, simply moving the body at that time is sacrilegious. Even an atheist who is empathetic can see that this moment matters to believers and resuscitation appears irrational and counter-productive. For EMS in this situation, we're committed to attempting resuscitation without a DNR. Some physicians believe an active DNR is one tool the elderly, especially the ill with limited time, should consider. We could show some consideration and reopen the conversation on the subject as a team to find a better way. This was done to produce our current protocol for "Withholding and Cessation of Resuscitation," and perhaps using newer technology such as telemedicine could help make quicker determinations.

This patient passed from the physical world to beyond in her house of God. For hundreds of years the Catholic Church has considered this moment, just before the attainment of eternal life with God, as the embodiment of their belief. To focus on only the physical aspect has always been considered sacrilegious. So, it is in many other faith traditions.

The areas I worked in New England were predominantly Christian. I served denominations including Roman Catholic, Protestant, Greek and Russian Orthodox, Mormons, Jehovah's Witnesses, and Christian Scientists. Most of us know Christianity as the monotheistic religion based on the teachings of Jesus Christ. Christians believe there is a need for spiritual care at the end of life and understand that science and technology cannot relieve all suffering during death.

In my experience, most Christians desire to have their last rights performed or prayers read for them by a church leader or family member at the last hour of their death. In others, especially when this moment is unexpected, their desire for services at home or on-scene may conflict with the need for transport to the hospital. But this is an opportunity to work with the patient and family, to reason what is the best decision for them at that time.

26 August 1992. The ranch style house is no different from the dozens that lined the street. Each house was identical right down to the same three cement stairs leading up to the doorway. The patient comes to the door clasping her chest complaining she is going to die. This is nothing new; we see this same scene all too often. We try to reassure and calm her, but she won't listen. Clearly the pain is unbearable. "Help me," she says as she drops to the floor. Luckily, my partner catches her. In the doorway, we scoop her up and put her onto the stretcher to the ever idling ambulance. As we work on her, she stops talking about her pain and looks one last time into my eyes before it the lights turn out.

CPR, BVM, Patient rhythm Course Fib, IV line in. I give a precordial thump with my fist to the sternum before an attempt with the electrical defibrillator, and her eyes light up again along with her vitals. Return of spontaneous circulation (ROSC). A precordial thump is a bit of an old school technique, used before defibrillation came along, but it's been proven numerous times to do the trick. The delivery must be quick as you see the rhythm; the speed of the thump leaves no time for the heart to go into a refractory state. I did it often because of my faith it would work and that I didn't need more electricity. That thump became a signature lifesaving tool for me, along with an ampule of sodium bicarb that always seemed to correct the chemistry. So, you see, science and faith can work well together.

In the early 1990's I had some saves using this technique only in a witnessed cardiac arrest in v-fib. The hospital doctors paid no attention. Seems they thought I was a young medic who thought too much of this antiquated technique—a fist in the age of electrical and medicinal solutions seems only dramatic. The medical journals confirmed that they were right, that there was no evidence this improved recovery but could not deny a difference in revival; however, my patients revived and often recovered well.

That patient went through her cardiac treatments that night and like many others needed to be transported to an advanced hospital to receive advanced cardiac care. The helicopter wasn't flying due to inclement weather—this was New England, after all—and the doctor waved me over. We transported her as a long distance IFT to Boston. With respect, I couldn't help but ask questions such as, "Do you recall the incident?" or "Do you remember when you were awoken?" The patients always seemed happy to talk about it given they now had the chance. The answers were often vague in detail, but many told me they felt confident that they were "going somewhere" or "leaving" and aware they had "come back" when they were revived. This was a common account. I don't consider the patients' experiences imaginary; they were clinically dead and can recall clear facts before and after. I consider the singular fact that they all know that they "left, went somewhere, and returned" as significant evidence that we're not simply a bag of flesh and bones that dies. We don't just *have* a spirit; we *are* a spirit.

PREPARATION:
A COMMON THREAD

I can't count how many elders I've seen "make their bed" as if unconsciously or preparing to die. I've seen it in my personal and professional life. You might have seen them as the quiet neighbor who seems so private and distant; then suddenly they pass away. You only noticed when you saw the ambulance idling in their driveway and, maybe later, a hearse. They usually keep to themselves and when the time is right they prepare their surroundings. All the of five faiths I mention here explicitly have unique approaches, traditions, and rituals based on their beliefs concerning what death is and how to handle it. For Catholics, life itself is the preparation. *But one common and colorful thread is that approaching this inevitable event is important and soulful.* Some focus directly on their religion but most cherish every worldly minute of time left. The differences among faiths are too complicated to describe each here. Instead, I will focus on the reflection that a life well lived is another common tradition.

12 August 1998. We arrive to find a centenarian who has laid herself perfectly supine in her bed, in her best dress with her cane and religious book by her side. She had already taken her last breath, as peaceful as an ocean breeze. It was her plan, and it was simply beautiful.

Her family is in the living room which is decorated with an array of family photos. The religious minister present. They called us to simply confirm her death before calling the funeral home—a common practice. I enter respectfully and discretely do my assessment without any disturbance of her or her surroundings. Upon leaving, the family allows us to stay a minute and shares their family photos with us, telling us some of their favorite memories of this woman. The deceased women had a celebrated life, a loving family, and had prayed persistently these last days and hours. The family was celebrating her life. The feeling in the house was soulful and magical.

The above scenario was not uncommon where I worked but could be contrasted with the less faithful scenario, which was all too common. I've seen many people who appeared to die faithless or alone, only a television for company. An entirely different feeling hangs in the air. It is hard to explain; it's certainly not peaceful. It appeared to me, going to these calls over the years, that dying with no faith in some spirit beyond, no religious path to prepare, and with little or no faithful companionship is a lonely and sad way to go. It is also a somber scene for family and friends.

I am not preaching or promoting any specific religion—only sharing an important aspect of my experience. Some people and their families are missing the glory of faith and support systems at times like these. I spent a great deal of time on scenes, often to support family members who seem lost. Unfortunately, in an area with a high elder population, a medic will spend more time in such situations than saving viable lives. *I believe tending to these people is an important part of the paramedic's job today because often there is no one else around for patient and family support.*

The days of the village pastor running over to the family farm, gathered around grandma are gone. Too many times I found myself alone with survivors, and at first I was at a loss as to how to support them. My partner would be putting our equipment away, and the police, if present, would not exactly be holding their hands. Some officers are incredible care advocates, but it's not typically their role. The reality is often no one would be there at the time of death. It is an inherited job that only certain individuals can do well, regardless of our uniform. It is also part of the mission I was proud of because there is a moral imperative to care for those who are grieving. But most don't get it. You can train whole classrooms of medics to render advanced life support, but is that the only type of support needed?

27 November 1990. On the long, straight, flat route through the west side of town, I watch the streetlights pass as I search for the side street. When I arrive at the house to confirm death for a family caring for a hospice patient, I wasn't expecting *more* patients. We enter the small ranch to find four family members gathered around their dad. The family explains he had been battling cancer, and with all the pain it is good to see him finally have some relief. They, on the other hand, are emotional, upset, struggling to find closure with his passing. My partner and I had gone through the few simple steps after confirmation of death; we had called the hospice RN and the funeral home. But the three children, who were in their forties or fifties weren't ready to part with their father.

I ask if they follow any particular faith or if there is a religious representative they would like to be present for proceedings.

"No, we're atheists," comes the defiant reply.

"That's fine," I say. "I'm only asking so I can assist you."

I am faced with people who seem to want to grieve, go through some closing ritual but have none and are now at a loss for what to do. I offer them the number to the local counseling team, suggest alternatively that they can talk with their doctor or the hospice RN if needed. Once again, their response is defensive posturing, as speaking with a professional about their loss would be a sign of weakness.

I recall it as such a sad scene. This family was so distraught, in tears even, but they had no clear path from grieving to healing. One minute they were stoic and the next they were asking me if I was going to stay a while and have some coffee.

This is where I think religion can make a difference, if not for the patient then for those they leave behind. What was needed here was not just a ritual or coping mechanism but something or someone to believe in. For those who believe that a religion is nothing more than a manmade program designed to serve man's need for structure, reason, and order, I would ask you take a closer look into the eyes of a grieving family such as this. For this family there would be no relief.

And we all know there are plenty of people who follow their religion out of tradition, loyalty, or habit but don't truly believe, which also offers no real comfort in such times. I could see that this family needed true belief in a higher power to reach a deep and meaningful healing. Any other manmade path (i.e., psychological counseling) organized to accomplish the same end would be no more powerful and enabling then their own efforts. In these moments, you can't always heal yourself; you need the power of a creator who knows how you're made in order to be truly healed.

So, there I am, up at night with them. There I am, there for them. As a simple person, I sit down nearby in the living room and am just quietly present. At times, they want to talk, and at times, the silence does the talking. Our dispatcher calls a couple times, and my partner explains our presence is needed at the scene as we may have a transport. Of course, we don't, but we need to stall the industrial machine to complete the more important job of helping a family cope with tragic loss. The youngest sits crying, shivering, and hyperventilating. I coach to slow her breathing rate.

"Watch the watch," I say, handing her my wristwatch. "Count the seconds, breathe in and out, slow. In, two, three, out, two, three. In, two, three, out, two three," I say in a calming cadence.

She does this, and the others watch and listen. The process is more than mechanical, it is graceful. It is done with the kindness of a brother. It is done religiously in that I am praying silently for peace for her, and it comes. Standing at the kitchen table there is a candle, which I focus on. She says her dad loved those candles.

"Maybe you should light it," I offer and she does.

I believe they can sense that this needs to be done, but this is not my job. It is for them to do. So, with time, the scene brightens with a small flame of hope, however quietly.

And so, we idle through the darkness of the moonless night back across the city.

20 March 1995. As we walk into the single family ranch house, I come face to face with Buddha, or should I say a two foot tall statue on a pedestal. As we are led through the house I cannot help but take in the religious symbolism. I can easily recall homes I've entered that are different from the others, and I always felt a little out of place like an alien in another world. It's often refreshing to see not all people have the dead savior hanging on a torture cross in their home. The home is decorated with colorful pillows and Tibetan Thangka embroidery scenes. There is a small Zen table gong, a wall plate etched with philosophical writings, and a small fountain in the corner lush with greenery.

I enter the room to find a frail elderly man who is dying. The lines on his face reflect his 90 years of life. His brow is furrowed, perhaps in some discomfort. I feel his weakened, thready radial pulses and listen to his diffuse lung sounds with my scope. As I place him on the cardiac monitor, his daughter enters the room.

"He is home on hospice," she says, "but I thought he was in too much distress. I'm just hoping he can get some relief." She hands me his DNR, which has no details beyond Do Not Resuscitate.

Glancing at his O2 saturation, I see it's at 84%. "Do you know if he and his doctor discussed him having a little oxygen to relieve his shortness of breath? Would that be alright?"

"Will that prolong his suffering?" she asks.

"I don't believe so; some treatments are warranted for comfort."

She agrees and says both her father and the doctor would then not mind. I place the nasal cannula on his face with some oxygen. I go through my series of focused questions on his most recent signs and symptoms relative to his condition, which was end stage renal disease. She shows me the powerful pain medication he is on. She tells me that he wants to be conscious of his thoughts as he passes away, so taking more heavy medication isn't in his best interest. We discuss different medications based on how much time he has left, maybe something to help him sleep a little if the doctor thinks he will not pass until tomorrow.

She calls the doctor on the phone. He and I speak briefly and then I hand the phone to her, being his guardian and health care proxy. We all agree on a plan to get him through the night comfortably but with respect to his religious call to be conscious and aware in his last hours. The overall feeling in the room is peaceful and spiritual.

In reflection, on this night and others like it, I couldn't help but notice some other differences that I found interesting. Now, mind that I'm speculating and not being critical of any religion; I'm fascinated and impressed by the morals of all. I noted that the overall tone of the house was peaceful and filled with the thoughts and sounds of that religion. One thing that was missing that I'm used to witnessing, being Christian, was the ritual sense of repentance, perceived by some as guilt or remorse for one's sins.

I understand the practice of repentance and bowing before God for forgiveness is critical to my religion's beliefs. I would not wish to imply that one is right or wrong to practice that ritual at such an important time but simply observed a difference that appears to set the tone during those final hours. It comes down to a matter of personal beliefs.

20 December 1995. I do not recall the priest's name, but I've picked him up a couple times from the church on the hill in the middle of the night. He clutches his Bible to his chest. He is in a great deal of pain and agony. I sense that the nighttime has compounded his physical and mental anguish. He sits perfectly straight on my stretcher. He is dressed as if he is going to give a sermon any minute. He has taken his medications but notes they are not helping. After my assessment, I try to be a supportive, friendly, but he is cautious and guarded about the details of what he is going through.

"He wants us to suffer," he remarks.

"You mean God does?" I ask, but he remains silent. "I guess the night intensifies this."

"Or the absence of the day," he replies.

"Well, I'm just an ambulance driver and don't know much, but I'm here to help. We could turn up the lights and read a psalm if you like."

Again, silence. But I catch a glance, maybe a grimace—a hint of appreciation for the gesture. He rests his head back, deep in his thoughts, looking into the dark distance out the back window.

There are several aspects of this patient's situation that I reflect on and can empathize with. The nature of his chosen profession, the responsibilities that come with it, and caring for a congregation mirror the problems he is facing alone in the middle of the night. Many older people have their medical problems amplified in the dark hours. Ironically, at night all medical services are closed, with their phone message "our business hours are Monday through Friday, eight to four." Friends and family are sleeping, not to be disturbed. It is also the time that a busy ER is at its busiest and shortest staffed with limited attention available for such patients.

There is no scientific explanation of why people suffer more in the night than the day. I laugh when I hear the medical experts try to explain it. "It could be several factors, lower anti-inflammatory hormone cortisol, lack of movement, circadian rhythm and the way nerves work…blah, blah, blah." All these excuses may point in the direction of *how* but not *why*. When those explanations fail, they tell you the reason is psychological—and that's when you know they don't have a goddamn clue. Physical pain, suffering, and non-physical suffering often intensify in the middle of the night, but I don't think there's a scientific explanation or a viable solution. I do believe we are more focused on ourselves at night because that's all we can see—the nature of our being and our soul.

WHO DO YOU
SAY WE ARE?

The established medical community does not believe that paramedics provide the same level of intellectual care as their facility bound counterparts. By this I mean experienced medics, in busy systems are adept at field assessments and can grasp more of the abstract situation than the medical academics at a facility. No offense intended or taken; they just think of us more as field transporters. The problem has been that we've lost out on communicating care with our patients as a team—as an extension of the entire system of physicians and staff to assess and direct all services needed. The receiving medical staff's perception comes from our limited time with a patient and subsequently our brief radio and verbal reports, which are simple and succinct. They have to be. But these are all they see and hear from one call as we come into the hospital. In our time on scene, the patients share more information in the safety of their home, which we are intelligent enough to gather, record, and share.

I contend some medics are actually more in tune with their patients in the community than other health care providers, even the patients' physicians. Just ask doctors themselves. They are bound by the walls of the hospital, time constraints set by a business driven schedule, and health Insurance requirements. They are forever sitting with heads bowed to computer screens, overbooked with patient admissions and discharge paperwork. For medical professionals in this environment, the depth of patient interaction is very limited.

As a medic, we are out in the community visiting our patients, making house calls, as routinely in some cases as doctors did a century ago. We are in patients' homes listening to their problems in real time, like a neighbor they can trust. In their home, people such as "Alice" in the next call share their problems more openly than in a doctor's office because we can see, hear, and experience the situation with her. For instance, we can see when the elder cannot walk to the kitchen and there is no food, when their medicine bottles are empty, and there is no evidence of visiting family. In contrast, at their doctor's office, the patient replies, "I'm walking fine," or "Yes, I'm eating well and have all my medicines." Over the years I have formed friendships with families whom I have repeatedly been called upon to assist, even requested by name. I've attended funerals and been invited to weddings and celebrations (although I usually decline out of respect for their privacy). But the point is that the relationship is there, with the trust, respect, and honesty that is earned in the interactions, and it is real, not based on a title or a business model.

When you walk into someone's home as a medic, time after time, and personally take care of grandpa or grandma, deliver Mom's child, then treat that same child over the years for everything from asthma or a bee sting to a fall off the bicycle, you can connect with the whole family. Isn't this healthcare at its best?

I can't count the times we've been to homes where people just want their medical concerns heard and wish for the knowledgeable medical liaison to be more of a neighborhood friend.

8 October 1992. We get the repeat 911 call for grandma Alice who says she needs Tom and Mike to check her condition; she's not feeling well. We have rolled over to this same small cape-style house weekly at the same time, 23:30, for the past month. It is always the same complaint, and our dispatcher is getting suspicious because we spend a lot of time there.

We walk in with only our basic gear because we know the routine doesn't call for advanced care. As we step in, I can smell fresh brewed coffee and see the baked cookies still warm on the table. We ask Alice, a widow who lives alone, how she has been, and she orders us to sit down and eat while she pours the coffee. Joining us she explains her routine ailments, from shortness of breath when walking to her anxiety about her daughters who left home many years ago. We listen and let her talk about everything from her church congregation to how the neighborhood and city has changed for the worse. We exchange family stories, and she tells us she hasn't smiled since we were here last Friday evening. Before we leave, we discuss her health and medications and give her a brief medical assessment. This is more a well-being and mental health check, which is every bit as important as some other calls. We never wasted much time at these calls, but we didn't turn our backs on the residents we served either.

We always referred people to their MD with respect, and it's not our job to play doctor. We don't have the knowledge or the technology. But the nature of it is we're out there, and when patients ask for information we provide it. We take time to listen to all the details of what ails them and observe contributing factors in their environment. We are not "technicians" with monkey skills working mindlessly or robotically all the time (most of us, anyway). Some of us are competent enough to comprehend and provide assistance in the community.

I consider many nurses and physicians my friends and have the utmost respect while bowing to their knowledge in their field; I prefer to work with them as part of a team. But most agree there is no single, cohesive community health care team. The agendas of the Nurses Union, the hospital and collegiate educational elitists, the Fire Fighters Union, and the growing "fly by night" EMS educational model don't align, and as a result, it has diminished the hard-won reputations of quality EMS providers. In other words, EMS providers don't go to college together, we don't train together, and we're not hospital based. Thus, we're divided. And a team that doesn't work together under the same coach is not a team at all. In the end, the patient loses.

Training at the College

My first job in EMS was with the city 911 service at Tapley Street in Springfield. It was a run-down, three room, two garage cinderblock building on the corner of a busy intersection in Springfield. I was instantly comfortable in the small dispatch room and drove the chair van. Conversation with the dispatcher, EMTs, and medics was easy and informative.

Springfield itself had had some nice old stores on Main Street like Johnson's Book Store and a drive-in A&W Root-beer restaurant mid-town. I lived in a tiny apartment by Forest Park and regularly saw my extended family members who lived down the road. Springfield was diverse and everyone worked together better than most communities. It was a working-class town. There was some crime, like any small city, but not much. I wanted to work in such a city because I saw the potential for a wide range of calls. I did not wish to sit idle in a small town nor be a number lost in a large city.

After my first day at Tapley Street, I visited the only basic EMT program in the area worth visiting. I heard Springfield College had a decent EMT course that would train me in all aspects of the job. On my first visit I found the instructors to be experienced, friendly and instructive. The program director wanted to know what my short and long-term goals were. At the time I wanted ultimately to work in a National Park as a ranger because I loved the great outdoors and bears—I liked bears. My short term goal was to be the best medic I could become. From what I had learned so far I would need a large volume of emergent calls, "rapid fire" responses to get all the experience hammered into me and learn from the most experienced out there. She confirmed I was at the right place at the right time.

The Springfield EMS system was not Boston EMS (by a long shot) or any big city for that matter, but it was a brand new and growing outfit. Starting fresh with relatively few medics per call volume made a great field internship. Similarly, the college had an international reputation. One of the professors founded a brand new paramedic program modeled on the most successful program curriculums out there, including Boston, Los Angeles, and New York City EMS. There would even be field rotations in New York City. With that, I decided I was in.

The EMT program was in its infancy and therefore relegated to the college basement, under a dormitory building. Yes, the bowels of the campus, which should have been a clue as to the shit I would be swimming in upstream for many fine years ahead. The programs classes flowed well from EMT to EMT-I to bridge into the Paramedic. The core skills were shared from program to program and the experienced instructors shared their knowledge. For example, we had instructors who had experience intubating patients in difficult scenarios such as in flipped-over car accidents, difficult to access industrial and construction sites, and in the streets during chaotic events. As soon as I learned to intubate and provide a needed airway, I was applying this in the field with some success. The intermediate program focused on assessing patients better and understanding other aspects of care before jumping into medications in the medic program.

My clinical experiences were eye-opening, with the full range of illnesses, injuries, and physicians involved. One of my patients was a sixteen month old admitted with bacterial meningitis; we administered antibiotics, and I mixed in a medication called dexamethasone, an anti-inflammatory to alleviate the swelling around the spinal cord and brain. The child noticeably improved and could begin to drink fluids in a day. I attended another two month old with a history of apneic events (spontaneously not breathing). I could see the familiar exhaustion in the parents' eyes, as I had witnessed my parents caring for an ill child. On 4/11 in the Emergency Room, we had a 24 year old who fell 25 feet off a roof during construction onto a barbed wire fence. He suffered an evisceration of his colon and laceration of his liver, which proved fatal in the trauma room. Despite rescue by medics and major resuscitative efforts by the trauma team to control the bleed, the damage to the liver was too severe. I was instructed hands-on how to perform open heart massage—although to me it was not so interesting given the outcome.

We had three pediatric surgeons from a group who came in for different cases from birth defects to hernias to wound care. The children's hospital cared for kids with every type of disorder including cancer up on the Children's Unit. I respected the nurses and doctors so much at Springfield Hospital that I decided to become an emergency room orderly. In that job I could assist more on the unit floors when needed. These kids were often out in their wheelchairs or walking with their IV poles and enjoyed talking about anything but their illnesses. Occasionally I brought comic books for them, but really they just wanted someone to listen, and the nurses needed a break.

Those years were a great time for me because I was always learning something new. I spent my days either working full-time, attending classes, or sleeping because I was exhausted. However, I learned a great deal assisting the Orthopedic Surgeon who came in for the broken bones. I learned to make plaster casts (yes, back then we put casts over braces) in the Ortho Room behind the Emergency Department. On occasion, we had to apply the Halo Gravity Traction for a person with a broken spinal cord. These are also used for children with scoliosis. The Halo Vest is applied to the person's thorax, and traction bars connected to the Halo are secured to the skull with pins. It looked frightening to be in, but it allowed the patients spine to heal. One 64-year-old female came in with compression fractures of cervical spinal discs C6 and C7. I assisted the doctor in applying the Halo Gravity Traction on her, but she couldn't stop crying, terrified at the prospect of having this metal cage mounted around her head onto her shoulders. The doctor had to be blunt: it was that or possible paralysis. Together, the doctor and I could be more optimistic and noted that this was temporary, and she had many years to look forward to of "walking in the park."

The Springfield Hospital Emergency Room was like a treasure chest guarded by the best characters. The staff there became a second family to me. The group was smart and talented. Certainly, there are great ER teams today, but the environment is more corporate, impersonal. Last time I worked at a hospital they had Disney administrators in to teach staff how to "smile for the customers." I feel sorry for students today; who have to learn about medicine as if they were in a television pharmaceutical advertisement, complete the voice-over warnings. I was fortunate to learn from staff who knew the technical jargon but could put it in layman's terms.

I remember we had a young patient who had split his entire outer ear in half playing backyard football. The pediatric surgeon was called-in to stitch this ear back together. Now, I have no idea why he didn't go to the surgical suite to operate, but he was determined we could do this minor surgery in a "suture room" in the back of the ER. The charge nurse, whose judgement I trusted more than anyone, had me assist the surgeon as she couldn't spare a nurse for such a length of time. I couldn't have been more excited or honored. We positioned the boy on the adjustable recliner and draped his head with a cloth. With only his ear exposed, we cleaned the hell out of it and began to work. It was here that I would get my first real lesson in patience. Starting inside the ear canal, I held the tissue together with two long metal clamps. The surgeon, slowly but efficiently, stitched the tissue together looking through binocular-like glasses. Stitch by stitch, occasionally pausing to sponge away the blood, the surgeon focused on joining the tissue back together seamlessly so there would be no scarring. We were in there for hours, finally finishing in the wee hours of the morning.

This same doctor had operated on my brother. My mom used to say that group of pediatric surgeons saved my brother's life, and they did. He had performed the "Nissen" operation to twist my brother's stomach into a knot, or valve, and then place a G-tube so my brother could get nutrition via liquid feedings. This is common today, but not so in the 1980's. Pioneer pediatric surgeons made life for my brother not only possible but bearable.

My experience in the ER also exposed me to all your garden variety general medicine: bizarre illnesses, gunshot and knife wounds, difficult to treat patients. I spent a great deal of time restraining people and putting-up with abuse. We endured long nights fighting with some of the evilest bastards that Lucifer could train. Some of these degenerates had histories of every deed that deserves incarceration. Abusers of substances, life, women, children, animals, and ER orderlies. They came in spitting, kicking, puking, bleeding, with shit blasting out their ass like it did from their mouths. Their language consisted of stringing together four letter words intermingled with odd vowels.

The only reason I mention this aspect is to emphasize that in working with the general public you need to learn patience. Managing the violence and the victims is not like managing a barber shop. No one sits quietly to wait their turn. Working in the city's largest Emergency Department and Trauma Center was basically the start of my clinical rotation which lasted years, not weeks, and thus made me a much better medic. I brought this first-hand experience to my classes. I shared my failures and successes and tried to include patients with complex psychiatric problems, but few of my classmates had the patience or experience to empathize and understand.

In the ER you learn to diffuse people—modifying your tone, using calming language, relaxing your body language. When that doesn't work, you learn to wrestle. Yes, wrestling became the team concept of restraining combative patients, which was not always possible due to short staffing. We had one patient attack us in the back hallway late one night. I came around the corner with our charge nurse, a tough no-nonsense woman, to find this guy throwing our security guard around like a rag doll. He picked the guard up off the floor, slammed his back against the stretcher railing, then threw him across the hallway into the wall like something on WWE. He actually bounced off the wall, leaving a guard-shaped dent. I wrestled the guy to the floor using a full nelson, but he gained force by using his legs, pushing me back against the wall. My trusty charge nurse took things into her own hands; she grabbed his hand and twisted, then his face twisted until his energy sapped out like a castrated bull. Another nurse came and threw on the leather cuffs, and we strapped him down tight to the stretcher. Our security guard was still rolling around in agony with a back injury that would haunt him for life. All this happened in minutes against a backdrop of patients yelling for their nurse, patients restrained in the hallway, a guy puking blood on the floor, and the staff performing ACLS in the main code room.

22 November 1988. Our orderly, Don, who is a bit brash but has a heart of gold is doing CPR chest compressions on a man of about 65 years of age. He is standing on a stool above the stretcher for leverage doing his typical forceful but perfect compressions. I hear the monitor beep with each compression from behind the dingy striped curtain in the patient bay. I go in to see how it is working or if Don needs a break. Behind the curtain, it's him, a doctor running the code, two nurses giving the medicines, and a respiratory therapist (RT) managing the airway with a bag valve mask. As Don does the compressions, the beep on the tracing becomes slightly more regular and an incomprehensible rhythm appears. The doctor tells Don to stop.

At that moment, the patient—who had been apneic and pulseless for some time—opens his eyes and awakens. The RT stops bagging ventilations into the man's mouth and the patient lifts his head slightly off the stretcher. He turned towards Don and lifts his hand, reaching out for a handshake. Don clasps the patient's outstretched hand. "Thank you," he says, looking Don straight in the eye. He lowers his head back down, breaths in and out, and the beeping rhythm fades to bradycardia. Then it flat-lines.

We are all speechless for a few seconds. The doctor orders more medicine and CPR to restart. The patient stays intubated for some time after but never again returns. An eerie silence falls over us. A clinically dead man had just come back to life to say "thank you" and show his appreciation with a handshake, only to depart this life for good seconds later.

It was a confounding experience. We had a glimpse of someone from the afterlife, or at least from somewhere on the stairway to it. What better experience to share with my medic friends who were all on this same journey with me? Or were they? I did share that experience at the college. Most tried to rationalize it, to find some scientific basis for this tiny miracle. It didn't seem to have the same meaning to them as it did me.

To me, this was it. I didn't have to become a doctor, priest, or professor to reach the pinnacle of professional life. This was proof positive that I was where I belonged on this spinning ball of dirt hurdling through space. I knew I was doing something that mattered, and no one could convince me otherwise. The way I figured it, *if someone took the time to come back from their final journey, out of this sphere on the way to the heavens, back to their very dead corpse, only to re-inhabit it for mere seconds, just to announce their gratitude for us and our sincere efforts; well then, this was undoubtedly a spiritual and important occupation.*

July 1989. We get a call to respond to a scene where a little boy, about four, had jammed a long thin wire hook into his ten-year-old sister's eye. My partner and I basically flew the truck to the scene. We skid past the end of their driveway, reverse back into it fast, and I leap out to assess the eight inch-long wire sticking out of the little girl's eye socket. The hook on the end had deflected off the eyeball globe and hooked up and over the top and behind the globe. We try to immobilize the crochet hook, but every time she looks around, the ten inch wire probes around like a long eyelash, hooked directly on the eye. I inspect under her lid hoping to see the hooked end sideways on top of the eyeball; no dice. We carefully and lightly support the wire as it moves on my finger. When we get her to the ER, the MD takes an x-ray to determine the position. The x-ray gives him a map of its position and he can remove it without issue or damage. The ER staff can finally breath and note that it is one of the luckiest things they have ever seen.

I think that there were forces at work here much more powerful than luck. This was nothing short of a small miracle. Let me break it down for us:

1. The child, although injured and in pain, finds the strength to not fall, faint, move, or pull on the wire hooked around her eyeball.

2. Her mother calls 911 and keeps her daughter still without panicking.

3. We speed over in a junk ambulance—that could barely start up reliably—in record time.

4. Assessing the girl in her house, she does not panic, and we form a strong rapport, working together and maintaining hope she won't lose her eye.

5. We cannot splint the moving wire for support. The weight of the wire hanging is placing pressure on the eyeball, so we learn that I must balance this wire on my finger as the wire moves around with her eye, which is hard to keep still.

6. We manage to load her on the stretcher, and together we balance this moving wire on my finger as we bounce over potholes. Eight miles for seventeen minutes.

7. Once inside the hospital ER, the physician has her head and eye socket x-rayed to see the position of the wire at that moment.

8. Without surgery, the doctor deftly manipulates the wire with delicate hand dexterity, first pushing in, then rotating it over the eye globe without any known damage.

9. The girl's beautiful eye is functioning and focusing properly. Miraculous.

I know I was praying, and I believe some silent prayers were at work here. This is not to say that if she lost the eye that it is proof that prayers don't work; rather, this story is proof that they do work when it is possible. Without that spiritual hope and faith in good works, miracles don't exist.

Working full time in the ER first and then transitioning in the field gave me a very wide lens view of what was happening. Being informed and knowledgeable is just as important; it makes the hospital/ field triage job easier and expedites the patient care transition in the ER. For example, I recall one night reading *Tabers* (a medical dictionary) along with a medical journal someone lifted from the hospital lobby. Some medics do this to pass time between calls. I was reading about childhood neurological disorders, including hydrocephalus (water on the brain) producing seizures. I had recently seen such a case in the ED and now better understood it after reading about it. That night I had a call for a pediatric patient with this rare disease acquired at birth. I had never had a patient in the field with that specific disorder before. When we arrived on-scene, the patient was recovering from a seizure, in minor distress, and the parents much more so. His mother told me he had hydrocephalus and began to explain when I politely replied that I thought I understood and confirmed the concerns inherent with that disease. For example, these patients often have visual problems, speech problems, headaches, and sleepiness, and those are often confused as lingering symptoms of their seizure. She was so relieved that a medic understood, and that increased her confidence and faith in us to help her son and transfer him into the hospital with the correct treatment.

One ER physician and long-time mentor, used to say that the word "physician" meant "to counsel as well as to practice." He felt it was his obligation to teach us medics a lesson or two for the benefit of his patients out in the community. He was one mentor that I acquired the practice of continuous learning by sharing. There is nothing more valuable in the field than shared knowledge, which is why I write. Some said we were just trained drivers but others had faith that we could apply any knowledge and skills taught to us and share what we learned. On this job, it is how and why we can help our patients' that determines who we are.

NEW YORK, NEW YORK

New York City, New York had a consolidating manner to offer in our paramedic training with people, plenty of people. I owe a debt of gratitude to my college and paramedic program professor for making it part of the curriculum. It was only one week in the spring and we were stationed in a different borough each day, but the experience of working with such outstanding people in a cement sea of sky scrapers was second to none. These experiences were more than clinical practice in the massive city, they were an immersion into multicultural communities on a scale that integrates you on all levels.

Our class checked into an old hotel in downtown Manhattan. We attended the NY-EMS orientation at their training quarters on Staten Island. It was a simple review of do's and do-not's and a ride-along with their paramedic crews. My schedule for the week had me serving Bellevue Station 13, Brooklyn, Kings County Station 33, 31, Coney Island, Harlem, and finishing in Manhattan. A typical day consisted of the following: take the subway to the ambulance station early in the morning, meet the crew, check the truck, post central, run the calls, attend the asthmatics, care for the cardiacs, alert for allergic reactions, code the codes, mop-up the MVC's, cautious of the cabs, down to the subway for the sullen, up the high-rise stairs for the heavy, pop the IV's in, push the meds, battle the buses, integrate with the insane traffic, call after call, return and reports, and stomp off in a stupor. It takes an extremely patient and dedicated person to work here. Many of the calls seemed innate to this massive cement city—an extension of the life of the city.

We had an undercover police officer whose legs were crushed against a wall by a car driven by a drug dealer. We think both his legs were broken and it was hard to see the man suffer so much while simply trying to do his job. I saw that theme repeated in New York: those trying to do their job versus those plying their trade in a game of survival.

In Harlem, a person jumped (or was pushed) out of a window several floors up to their death below on the pavement. The crowd gathered quickly and was beginning to get riotous. I didn't understand. An armored police vehicle arrived on scene for riot control. They brought along EMS providers, and there was nothing we could do, so we retreated back to the metro area to get some pizza.

In Manhattan, a man with chest pain (CP) was being treated in his doctor's office three floors below ground. We rode with the stretcher on the escalator because the elevator was busy. Once in the MD's office, the doctor explained the patient's symptoms and that he had done an electrocardiogram (EKG) and given aspirin. I determined the man had tachycardia and treated him. I called in to our central Medical Control (MC) for orders for morphine sulfate and a medication to break the tachycardia. This concept of *one* medical control physician located centrally and available only for medics prehospital was new to me. Back home, your medical control physician was one of several MDs working in the main hospital and therefore busy with patients, as well. Our NY MC was there for me; he listened carefully to exactly what I described. He understood without question and gave me orders for 10+ mg of MS PRN along with the anti-dysrhythmic med. I treated our patient right there in the doctor's office, packaged him up, and transported him up to our ambulance in the street.

We had a high-rise fire on the corner of Fifth Avenue. The mass casualty vehicle was a converted school bus. The building was a short, brick apartment complex. Luckily, no residents were hurt, but several fire fighters received minor injuries—cuts and burns to the hands, physical exhaustion, smoke inhalation, and heatstroke. I treated them in this converted mini-hospital unit, which seemed fairly low-tech for such a task in one the country's biggest cities. But it did the job, and everything we needed was there. The fire fighters extinguished the fire and before I knew it, we were standing around on Fifth Avenue while they secured the building. It was just after five, and I was advised by my fellow medics to watch for the parade about to come down the sidewalk. I had no clue what that meant. Then, like a stampede, dozens of business women impeccably dressed came speed walking down the sidewalk in their sneakers while carrying their heeled shoes and business bags. They were leaving work and making the mad dash for home.

The treks up and down the city, literally from subways to skyscrapers, put in perspective just how many people there are here. You can sense they know they're not all special but cooperative for such a mass of humanity, and I found them to be generally considerate. That may sound cynical, but it is a fact: you cannot save everyone when there are millions to help. You can only do your best one patient at a time. In effect, this awareness relieves you of some pressure. Call after call, up and down these massive towers, we search for those people in need, and it is very satisfying to provide personal care in such an immense, crowded, and impersonal place.

In New York City an ambulance is called the "bus" because they run all over the place like cabs and buses. Calling one is not much more exciting than ordering a cab (or a pizza) with about the same level of expectation. The New Yorkers I met seemed to me much more composed, reasonable, and poised at scenes. Usually, the response times were between one and seven minutes (fantastic), and if we were delayed, a patient might casually remark, "I know you guys must be busy or the traffic jammed." There also seemed to be more trust in the medics given everyone could see them working in the streets every day. Working in the big city worked for me. I was hooked. On my last day I only wanted more.

That Friday night on the rig, I asked the crew to swing by my hotel on the west side. I went into the lounge and found my professor enjoying a beer and listening to the students' stories and experiences after the long week had ended.

"Can I stay for the weekend and ride with the Manhattan crews?" I asked him.

"The whole weekend, by yourself?" the professor replied.

"Yes, I'm with good crews and would be extra careful," I said.

"You wouldn't be covered under the college's insurance, you know. You're all on your own if something goes wrong or you get hurt."

"I understand. I promise, I'll be my best."

"OK, Thomas, good luck."

And with that I was out the door and back on the bus. All my fellow comrades were celebrating the end of their week drinking and partying. Not me, I wanted to be back on the bus and meet more NY patients. I rode around the clock through Sunday and headed for home. During those hours, I learned a few tricks from the medics and the New York system. Run after run (or job after job as they would say), I met my patients, established rapport, accelerated assessments, initiated care plans, and treated my patients quicker and easier than ever. I learned how not to make a big deal out of simple tasks like popping in intravenous lines or placing endotracheal tubes. The bottom line was not to get tunnel vision—get it done and care for the patient. The patient: how can you not focus on the patient when there is a vast sea of millions here?

LITTLE PEOPLE

21 July 1989. My partner is a nurse who was fond of listening to herself talk. Some of our group doesn't care much for that, but I listen and learn because, hell, she is smart and on the inside working with doctors; and she has experience with pediatrics and neonates. Now on neonates, honestly, I am a new medic, so despite my experience in the ER, when looking at a neonate I might as well have been looking at a little alien. We spend the morning talking about neonates and the physiological differences that set them apart from adults when it comes to assessment and treatment. Most importantly, we discuss their tendency to crash quicker than adults because of their small fluid volumes and therefore the need for rapid IV access and fluids early in treatment. Intravenous access on a neonate can be like threading a needle into a piece of angel hair pasta rolling around under thin cellophane. I tell her about the crash course I had recently on a non-emergent neonatal transfer.

About a week before this shift, I transported a neonate in an isolette incubator from a small community hospital to Springfield Hospital. The hospital team we brought with us consisted of the specialized pediatrician, RN, and RT (Respiratory Therapist). On these NICU/IFT's (Inter-facility Transports) the teams were excited to go out with us and more than willing to train us in tricks of their trade. This was still the 80's so people were more open to sharing ideas to help one another—before everyone got their head so deep up their political asses like today. On that call the newborn needed IV access, and they had to insert the IV into the scalp vein. The RN allowed me to assist by holding the infants head and prep the scalp as she canalized the vein with a tiny butterfly needle. The process was simple if you took it step by step, but I had rarely seen these done in the ER. On each of these runs with the little ones, I learned something new from the team.

Back to the day in question. That afternoon the calls begin to roll in, and we respond to a north end neighborhood for a child seizing non-stop for over an hour. We roll our lumbering Braun rig right up to the apartment door. The dad is outside looking fairly stressed, showing that edge of urgency to get us inside. The mom had her newborn premature infant on the couch—seizing away, grand mal. We pull-off a couple layers of clothes to find the little alien burning hot with fever. We start a steady cool down with moist towels. His vitals are elevated, but the child is dry as a bone; he had not taken in any fluids by mouth recently. We both search the arms and hands with nothing showing or palpable for an IV.

"Hey, shit for veins here, this looks like a scalp or he has nothing," my partner says.

"We can just ride him over. We're fairly close, but he doesn't look good does he?"

"No. I'm going to get the monitor and cot," she says, dashing out the door.

I am left with our first-in bag which has the IV kit and O2. I try counting his heart rate at the brachial; too tachycardic—an empty tank.

"OK, let's give him some fluid," I say as I yank the kit from my first-in bag and pull out the 25-gauge butterfly needle and supplies. Now, I thought, this is not protocol, and if I blow this vein and cause a hematoma, the doctor's going to be ripped. But if I bring him over in this shape—seizing or worse, maybe he crashes—that doesn't work either. Most importantly, I couldn't just sit there and watch him seize, burning up brain cells.

"Hey madre, habla inglés? ¿Sí? Hold...agarro...el cabesa. Like this, sí?"

As his mom holds his head, I find the perfect vein about an inch from the top of his head. I prep the site and carefully insert the thin needle into the angel hair pasta vein followed by a careful syringe flush from my charged loop.

"Perfecto. Al dente, eh?" I say.

His mom just looks at me, puzzled. *Why is this white guy happy he stuck a needle in my child's skull?* she seems to be thinking. I secure the site with a dressing and tape as my partner walks back inside, monitor in hand.

"What? You did it without me?" she asks. Happily, she connects our small bag of saline and begins the flow with an added squirt of Valium to chill the tremors.

We bring the little one into to the ER, met with odd looks from the staff. After a few minutes of questions, criticisms, and some reasoning, it is accepted as a success.

It may not sound like a big deal but at the time in our little world it was a big step for the local prehospital providers. After all, the system was relatively new and now a medic who had learned a skill from a hospital doctor, not typical in our protocols, had applied that skill without orders to help a patient on the scene. If we could do this, what was our limit? Our training involved some time in NICU and PICU but not nearly enough.

Later in my career, I was one of the few in the field to recognize this gap in training, so when I ran a hospital-based EMS service, I made it mandatory that medics spend at least one 8-hour shift in NICU and PICU as part of our critical care recertification. This was well worth the effort not only for patient care; we also made progress elevating prehospital providers' reputation.

2 July 2002. A call comes in for a seven-year-old hit by a car. As we motor down the road to the scene, my partner notes that I seem calmer than others given the nature of the call, and I just nod. Anxiety and drama have no place in EMS. The young boy was found by his mother, who is hysterical—understandably. She is holding his head, which thankfully isn't bleeding that much. A quick look at the top of his head reveals his skull was in fact split in half, superior top to posterior, clear break of the bone revealing the brain, which is intact. Knowing the different bones and sutures of the brain case matters not a bit out here. Our job here is to hold it together and get them to the surgeon alive. I try to get a two second understanding of the mechanism: if his head was hit or run-over but the scene is too chaotic.

The boy is in shock and wide awake, looking at me as I hold his skull together. We manage to get him on a long board with a KED device to keep his body and spine mostly in-line. At the back of the ambulance, his mom is babbling, crying, praying, which seems to frighten the child more than his head injury. I encourage her to keep praying, calmly—for strength, for the boy who needs that more than anything at this time. Children who are injured need our lead of confidence. The boy looks up at me in agreement. I tell the boy to hum a song he likes. "How about Silent Night?" I suggest, and he begins to hum the tune.

Delivered

9 April 1991. Suburb of Springfield. A young couple speeds down Park Ave headed for the bridge to the hospital. The wife tells her husband she isn't going to make it. The baby is on its way. He turns the car around and heads for the Donut Shop; he tells her he thinks he saw a cop car there. As they swing into the far side of the shop, they spot our ambulance and pull in next to us. I hop out to see the woman has started pushing and lifted her legs to allow the inevitable birth of her child. I open the passenger door just in time to catch the infant as he comes out. We swaddle the lively child and place him on his mom's chest, who is now comfortably on a stretcher in the back of the ambulance. She says she did not know how this would all turn out, but she prayed to find someone to deliver. We delivered.

I've delivered over a dozen children in the field without much assistance and assisted on over a dozen other deliveries. It is different in the field compared to the hospital—uncontrolled, more natural one might say. For most medics including me there is the messy aspect; of course, it's a purely physical function. However, in so many minutes the mess is over, and looking into the eyes of newborn life, life that has just arrived on our planet and taken its first breath, can be magical. I was never thrilled to be there at first, but then in a moment suspended in time, the child opens his eyes, and you know they're seeing you in this world for the first time. Their big eyes focus on you as if to ask, "Who's this?" Absolutely amazing.

After some of these child deliveries there would usually be a follow-up conversation. More than once I took the opportunity to discuss opinions on the bigger issues of life, like where it derives from, creation vs. random order, and God. Most agree on the idea of the miracle of life, but it is a difficult conversation for some. Despite delivering newborns, some medics refuse to recognize them as God's creation or plan for creation, especially when something bad happens such as birth defects. I can understand that. To me, God *creates* order out of chaos. We try to imitate that such as an artist who paints a picture. It is not easy and it does not always come out perfect but it is still a creation.

PEOPLE WHO NEED PEOPLE

Twenty-four hour shifts, two to four shifts a week, shift hold-overs, seventy-two to one hundred plus hour weeks, ten to twenty-four calls a day, non-stop until you're burnt out. Beginning in the mid-80's, EMS became the new American industrial sweatshop. Our government took a step back and allowed the private sector industrialists to take the helm. With non-medical opportunists piloting the private ambulance services with only money in mind and corporate strategies to play the system, we, the dedicated care-takers, didn't have a chance to improve care as we wanted. That requires investment. Most companies were far too happy to drive that ship into the ground in the name of profits. I found a few companies years later who invested in the operations for better care, but for most this was about volume, numbers and money, not people.

My class was the second to graduate from the local college. We were eager to apply our new skills and fight the good fight. Some students went onto to "bigger things" or back to school. But some of us we wanted to stay and work the city we lived in and cared about. Thus, years later, I felt it best to become a supervisor and then manager to guide the team while promoting our work; certainly no one else had our backs. I dabbled in the management "arts" and took more classes, but I was too involved in the field to sit behind a desk for long. So, for the first ten years I worked and lived on the street, serving the greater good and anyone else who dialed those three numbers: 911.

My life was set to a soundtrack of ringing and chirping—a phone, pager, or beeping radio to get your ass in gear and respond to another crisis in the middle of the night. It was enough to grate on your nerves after a while. I slept sitting upright in the idling ambulances with 400,000 plus miles on their tired engines and broken frames, all while I inhaled the poisonous CO fumes pouring out of the engine housing like incense.

In those years, I did thousands of responses. Take an average of one call every hour or two (12-24 shift). That's 24-48 a week minimum (1,200 - 2,400) a year plus OT shifts). That is literally tons of people to lift, to take care of—a dizzying number of responses and patient interactions. I watched medics join and quit one by one, amounting to dozens lost, so after a while I gave up learning names. Some die-hards stayed for lost causes or the same stubborn values as mine. How I kept my sanity all those years I may never know, but I do know some help from above was there during the worst hours. A strong characteristic of my job that motivated me is autonomy—the freedom to be self-reliant in the face of challenges. For the long haul and at scenes like a multi-casualty incident (MCI), a cohesive team is important. At times like these, you depend on your coworkers and they depend on you. So for how long, to what extent, and do the people who call for your help always need you?

30 July 1991. We lay sleeping on our bunks in our upper Boston road garage when we hear the gunshots echo from downtown in the distance. Upright, we sit looking at each other's shadow in the dark.

"You hear those?" my partner asks.

The phone rings. Shots fired, downtown intersection, woman and a baby shot front seat of the car. We scramble upwards and hustle out to the waiting rig. We cruise down the main drag at a fair clip while watching for pedestrians or cars pulling out of nowhere.

We know the location is down the street from the police department, and we arrive to find an empty car riddled with bullets. The officer on-scene says the mother and child were both shot by a man who fled; the victims were raced away by police who thought it quicker to run them a mile down the road to the hospital trauma room. We are relieved they have been transported, having seen too many shot that summer.

We slowly shuffle back to our rig and begin the paperwork as "canceled on scene." Moments later another call: an assault with a knife. So much for getting a break from the residual of the rotten.

We roll up to the old Victorian house turned rental building with no police in sight yet. A tall man walks over holding his left side like he has a stomachache. We pull out the stretcher to the ground, quickly set it up for him to sit, lift and roll him into the box. I jump in and hit the bright overheads so I can see my subject. He's laughing and pulls open several layered shirts to reveal a one-inch hole pumping out bright red blood underneath his rib cage. I grab a trauma pad and hold pressure while gliding my stethoscope over his chest wall with the other hand to listen to breathing. He says he got stabbed but "no big deal." He shows me dozens of scars from past knife and bullet wounds all over his chest and back he received while in his home country far away but not long ago.

We start rolling over the small hill of the city, down Chestnut Street. I pop-in a couple large IV's and flow some fluid. I enjoy the lofty nature of this guy as he laughs at his situation. He never shows any emotional or physical stress. He tells me he was named after his grandfather. He's got spirit, and it appears to have held him aloft through all of his conflicts. I had taken notice of the Christian cross he wore and we talk as I hold a trauma dressing against his bleeding wound.

"Are you a Christian," I ask.

"I am," he says. "In my country we are of many faiths."

He seems to appreciate my recognition of his faith, and we talk about his hometown and his family there. He had found work here and sent money back. I learned more about him while holding pressure on his stab wound than if I were sitting next to him in a coffee shop or bar.

I learned not to judge individuals or group members based on the crimes of a gang—or any cultural group. I have seen brutality in them all, but I have also seen kindness, faith, humanity. So, the question is how can a medic do better on these calls? The only thing I could figure was to treat everyone with the same respect, show them how we could help without judgement, and recognize any good if and when we saw it. Many of these people came from extreme poverty but were rich in spiritual health. I grew as a person, as I learned to work and communicate with diverse people from different cultures.

Proverbs 14:31. "He who oppresses the poor shows contempt for their Maker, but whoever is kind to the needy honors God."

I could write an entire book, as some medics have, of the rotten scenes we had to go to, from beatings and rapes to murders. But once again, I'm trying to avoid pointless war stories and giving those battles too much credit, but to ignore them completely wouldn't be fair to those patients who needed our help. Our efforts often made a difference. Treating *every* patient like they were my brother or sister made that difference. That's not easy when someone is yelling at you, sometimes in another language, or punching, kicking, or even shooting at you.

"People who need people are the luckiest people" is a line from a famous show-tune. (So, maybe it has some merit.) For those who are considering a career as a medic in a busy 911 system, I would like to be honest—because most paramedic programs are going to gloss over this aspect. Working with the general public and dealing with people has its challenges. People are complicated—though some bad behavior may be explained by psych 101 theories, others are confounding. We highly recommend those psych classes to understand those inherent disorders, behaviors, thinking and functioning that are not in one's control; so we can help everyone as I have. But in using your inherent, uncommon sense you will find that all the scientific jargon and religious reasoning will not explain the ridiculous human behavior and intentions you will have to live through in a busy system.

26 July 1993. My partner and I respond to a woman unconscious in a neighborhood off Bay Road. We go to the second floor of the small apartment house to find a middle-aged woman unresponsive with a blood glucose of ten. She's supine on the kitchen floor, breathing sufficient with snoring respirations and stable vitals. She was mumbling before we arrived, apparently asking for some water. Her teenage son heatedly tells us she was thirsty, and he had gotten a cup of water.

"I need to give her this now. It's what she needs, don't you know that?" the clearly frustrated teen emphasized.

"Yes, I understand, and you can give it to her once she's awake again," I reply. "Right now, she's unconscious so we're going to give her some fluid and sugar through an IV, which should wake her up."

"She would still be awake if you got here sooner. You took too long. Now look at her."

"We know you're frustrated, and we got here from across town as fast as we could. So, I'm asking you let us do our job."

"F-ing assholes, man, you took forever."

I let it go.

I assess the patient, open my IV kit, and assemble my IV start kit while he is cussing us out. I apply the tourniquet, locate and cleanse the A/C vein, and place the tip of my 16g angio on top of the vein ready to veni-puncture, ready, steady—smack! A cup of ice cold water hits my face followed by a barrage of four letter words, of course.

Our patient's son had grabbed the cup of cold water off the counter, turned quickly, and threw it with all his effort right in my face. Why? Just because he thought he had the right, I guess.

With water dripping off my face onto the patient's forearm, I exhale and pause. "OK, J see. Please get him out of here," I say to my returning partner.

No water had landed on the needle or site, so I took a breath and without delay, place the needle in the vein. I let the saline flow and give her Dextrose until she regains consciousness. When she comes around enough to talk, she gives me a strange look.

"Why are you all wet?" she asks me.

"It was a little hot in here," I say.

Getting her out was not easy either; she was over 360 lbs. and could not walk. We had to lower her down the stairs in a Stokes basket, to which her son had more to say but nothing to throw at me. The patient awoke and, seeing her son upset, became concerned. The neighbors came out distraught, the police appeared bothered, while their dispatcher was impatient with the scene time, and the firefighters frowned with lifting and lowering the heavy stokes basket. The tune played in my head as we went down the stairs, "People... people who need people... are the luckiest people... in the world..."

So, we try, repeatedly, to show some empathy. We start with the simple, universal, "Are you okay?" Next, the "Let's fix this" approach as we examine their cut, bruise or bullet wound. I learned to include the patient in their own treatment as it changes their mindset, say from anger and retaliation, to focus on repair and healing. I would ask them to hold the trauma dressing on their wound or the gauge of the B/P cuff as I took their blood pressure. When operating the monitor, I would have them hold their own EKG strip and read it with them. Even if we don't speak the same language, everyone understands a thumbs up or a concerned pointed finger at the rhythm strip.

In talking with people who are suffering or dying in violent circumstances, it did help to refer to faith at times. It may sound futile—and most medics would certainly not "waste their time"—but I found it helpful over the years to recognize and read people by how they respond to questions with key words. So, if the guy on my stretcher who has been shot three times is losing consciousness, and he expresses *his concern* with dying, I might ask about his faith while I work to stop the bleeding.

10 July 1990. A 15-year-old male shot in the chest, thorax, and abdomen, heavy blood loss, quickly losing consciousness. I'm alone treating him in the back of the ambulance. He has massive bullet entrance and exit wounds pulsing out blood.

"Man, am I dying?" he asks.

"I'm trying to prevent that."

He's struggling to breathe, grappling all over the stretcher. I'm applying pressure to his wounds but the blood continues to pour out and the ambulance floor is now a skating rink of deep crimson red.

Gasping for air, he rips off his oxygen mask and stares into my eyes, looking ghostly gray and tired beyond his years.

"Need your help. Do you have any faith?" I ask.

"I do, I do… Jesus help me. Oh my God, help me…" the boy says moments before he slumps back against the ambulance wall. In a few seconds, he dies.

It is hard to put into words (and impossible for actors to portray on film) these last moments of this young man's life, an all too common scenario in America. He knew he was dying. He decided to talk about his faith in Jesus in the last seconds of his life. What I can't put into words was his appreciation that I asked that question, which gave him the freedom and confidence that he could say his peace before he died.

A critic will read this and say I'm inferring conclusions without concrete evidence. Forgive me, but we didn't have time for a thorough interview and detailed last rights ritual, but I think he said it all. Spirituality and religion matter in the end. I don't need to make a grand argument for applying spirituality over science because I trust in both—though one more than the other. I love science and medicine and believe faith in treating humankind has merit, but it's even better if inspired by faith in something greater.

As for all the conceited "scientific faith" based ideologies and solutions, I wouldn't bet my life on them. I often read the claim in medical journals that their studies are rational because science is demonstrably superior for getting at truths about the natural world. Tell me, what is the truth in this last case? I guarantee they would say a surgeon could have saved him, but I have placed hundreds of kids like this before trauma surgeons who only cut them up like a frog in a high school anatomy class. Surgery can be miraculous, but not alone. What an atheistic scientific brain cannot understand is that was not what this boy wanted; this young man knew he was dying and wanted his holy communion, not a transplant. That is it: the Truth.

The 80's and 90's saw a rise in scientific and technical developments that impacted the field—better vehicles and monitoring equipment, readily available CT scan and MRI machines, for example. I emphasize that I have always liked the science. Still, my main interest always rose to a higher calling. Ultimately, the science bored the hell out of me because it let down people in the end.

As I began my career in EMS, I assumed it wouldn't be long before I moved on. Along the way I learned much from my interactions with the communities I served. With patients, I often found our interactions short and intense but, in these cases, not superficial. To me, they were profound. Could we have meaningful relationships with people whom we only saw for minutes? Do people really need people? I found we need each other, but if it's not in mutual respect of our faith or God, then what for?

PURGATORY

Returning to my relatively compact city of Springfield, I was ready to take on anything. I had spent time in the Big Apple and one of the best EMS systems in the country, so surely I could handle this small campfire. Check the truck, prep the gear, go. If I had known what I was going to witness over the next few decades, I would have quit on the spot.

God works in mysterious ways. We take on tasks like setting out on a mission; yet we can never be truly prepared. I think when we are so young, naïve, or stupid, we just take responsibility (some of us.) We simply cannot fathom the volume and intensity of experiences that assault our senses in such a role. The early 1990's were especially hard with the violence peaking in Springfield and all of Massachusetts (40,239 incident of violence reported to police); the same was true for the nation (1992-1993 had the highest volumes of violent crime in the USA, period from 1980 to 2005.)*No report notes why. So you prepare yourself to handle the violence but those are not always the hardest cases to manage. Each case is like another brick added to your backpack, and sometimes the first brick feels the heaviest—like when your first call is for a pediatric code, and there are twenty three hours and as many patients remaining in your shift.

06:52. 7 August 1992. "Child found by mom not breathing" is the call. The previous crew has no time to give us a shift report. They hand us the keys and off we accelerate to the city's center, Mason Square area. We round the corner and see the mom holding a little blue baby high up in the air over her head like a sports trophy. We can see the infant is not breathing, and the mom has tears flowing down her cheeks. It's the end of her world. I feel for her, and my sole focus is to bring this child back. She hands me the baby before I even have time to put on gloves. The baby is cool and moist and very limp and heavy. I swing around and place him on the stretcher to begin our ALS treatment. It isn't looking good. I'm ventilating him through an endotracheal tube, but his color isn't changing to pink after a minute of bag valve ventilations. My partner has him on the monitor, and the green flat-line streams across the screen to say there is no electrical activity here.

I look out the side door where his mom is still standing there trembling, her hand over her mouth, and her huge brown eyes flowing tears.

"Easy mom, easy," I say. "We're still working here," trying to give her hope.

I quickly refocus on the child, assessing head to toe. *Now think, think.* I look for any signs. I go over the ABC's (airway, breathing, circulatory). What could be the cause? Choking, aspiration, asthma, cardiac, position, sudden infant death syndrome (SIDs)? I ask the mom, "Any problems last night—breathing problems, wheezing, cardiac, temperature, vomiting, been lethargic or ill lately?" To each she shakes her head no. "What position was he found in?" No answer.

I double check the ET tube, auscultate all lung fields, pop in an IV line, ad flow the fluid, push the epi before the line is even taped, add alkaline sodium bicarb and salt, and he's still lifeless.

With Mom now wailing outside the door, she knows this is the end as we're not giving her hopeful news. At this moment I want to roll the rig over to the church down the block. Now that would be helpful. I think, *call her friends and family, and get the reverend there.* It's a beautiful white church and we could roll the stretcher in and gently place the child in a velvet lined cradle and join our voices in a song. Maybe some Gospel glory: "Abide with Me, Jesus Promised," or the modern version of "I Can Only Imagine." I believe that would be good, that would be something. Better than a cold cot at the hospital ER followed by the morgue. That would not be a good treatment for our second patient here, the mother of the child.

But reality sets in. The three of us know it's time to transport to the hospital, as required. I'm in the tech seat at the head of the stretcher, and I look over to the mom who stands a few feet from me, leaning in the side door.

"Do you want to be seated up front?" I ask, as it is a policy.

She cries and shakes her head in a determined "no." She will not leave her child's side. I have my partner ventilate while I set out and assist her into the box with me to sit right next to her baby as we ride in.

I tell my partner before he goes up front to drive, "Take it slower and e-a-s-y, keep the speed and noise down; that will be much easier on her."

My partner knows that this mom's our patient too; we need to care for her because we can, and that is the best we can do now. Down the road we roll, side by side, quietly, not a journey for the faint of heart.

I never minded these emotionally difficult calls because I saw in them a higher purpose. They are one reason why I chose this job: to be there for good folks who need me at the worst moment of their lives. I would not want some crew of fools serving that mother and child heartlessly, mechanically. That one moment in time can define the rest of the day for me, life for her, and put everything in perspective, however hard it is to see.

The calls keep coming in over the radio; sometimes before you're even finished at the hospital with your current call. All day and into the night. Seventy-eight year-old female with shortness of breath; 67 y/o male with chest pain; 14 y/o asthmatic teen; drunk 52 y/o who fell off his bicycle waiting for the light to change; 42 y/o who sliced her hand cutting vegetables; multi-car MVC with multiple injuries. I consider each person as they endure their own emergency and I think, *This is their injury, no matter how big or how small. It has upended their life, and they're looking for someone who cares enough to tend to them.* And you can find patience and forgiveness to care for each one if you always remember that first call of the day; it streams through your mind like a silent film.

I mumbled a silent prayer for that mother as I would for many. Sometimes I needed a moment of peace between runs. It's hard enough to be a mother with a sick child, but to lose a child at a young age must be devastating.

20:06. 18 October 1992. Call for a 30-year-old female in crisis, suicidal ideation (SI) at home in her kitchen. We approach with a police officer up the fire escape to the third floor. The officer pushes us aside to enter first, weapon drawn. The woman has a large kitchen knife and points it at him threatening to stab him. Her face is twisted into a clenched grimace; she is clearly not in her right mind. Standing behind the officer and looking down the sight of his gun leveled at her chest is a tense moment. The officer talks her down, deescalating the situation. We join him, gaining her trust, and she puts the butcher knife down. Her anger dissipates as she becomes convinced we are not a threat.

I understand that her perception is her reality. She brandished the knife because she knows that there are real threats, even from herself. As first responders, we understand that and convey our deep concern for her in the tone of our voices. The police were there on this scene. The public perception that the police carry a gun just to protect themselves and shoot "the bad guy" was false. Sometimes these weapons were used as restraint devices, to stop an assault because that is all they had that was effective. New devices became available such as mace, pepper spray, rubber bullets, stun guns, tasers, tethers, etc. They rarely needed any of those; we always de-escalated the patient verbally. I had a renewed understanding and respect for the police after these situations. My job was stressful, but I didn't have to worry about killing someone. That officer knows that if he was *forced* to pull the trigger of his weapon, it would affect him for life. Especially for patients with mental illness, the use of lethal restraint is not acceptable. No doubt, when it's you or them, action needs to be taken, but we always found a way without weapons. Regardless, you always hope to disarm them peacefully and gain the opportunity to do the good work. That said, I learned to always be aware because if a patient was willing to stab me on-scene, they're not completely harmless once disarmed and on the way to the hospital.

The assessment that follows reveals of history of physical and mental abuse that has driven her to near psychosis—an all too common pattern. On the ride to the hospital, I give what little support she will tolerate. I'm cautious; there is a delicate balance when you're providing care in such a situation. While I'm absolutely empathetic and supportive on the one hand, I can't be obsequious as she will perceive that as insincere. I could sit there quietly like some medics and only ask minimal medical questions, but that's useless. On the other hand, I can speak *with* the patient as a concerned friend or brother would—listening more than talking, truthful, transparent, just a few words at a time in low tones. The goal is to understand what could be helpful for them. For example, is there a past or present friend or therapist the patient would like contacted? I learned not to inquire specifically about family. I learned to choose my words carefully. When and where was the last time things were good? Can we get you back to that place?

There is almost never a time to bring faith or personal beliefs into assisting crisis patients in the field. But I think the characteristics of faith in the provider are very helpful to these patients. These happen to be similar values as those expressed in psychiatric care. A few examples are when we convey a sense of self-worth to the patient, a form of Grace, that life is a gift; the communal characteristic that we're all together in this life; the characteristic of forgiveness, that there is no fault on the part of the patient, which can be made palpable without even talking. These three, just sensed in conversation, can make a patient feel better compared to a medic sitting there just observing the "sick patient."

Studies of these personality characteristics have shown an overall positive effect of spirituality in psychotherapy. A published study on Religious Cognitive Emotional Therapy (RCET) has proven that basic religious beliefs can help people find the meaning of life and resolve their identity crises.

05:00. 18 September 1991. Call for an elderly female with chest pain. We walk into a well-kept home to meet an eighty-something year-old woman sitting in her chair in her living room. Walking over to her, the carpet is so soft there is no noise. She looks miserable, and that concerns me. A girl, maybe eleven or twelve, stands next to her holding her hand. I introduce myself, kneeling down to her eye level.

"What is happening this morning?" I ask.

"My granddaughter here thought I should call because I'm having some chest discomfort. I was going to see my doctor later this morning."

"OK, do you know what's causing it?"

"No, but my heart feels as though it is racing."

"Can you describe where the pain is?"

She points to the center of her chest as we assess her vitals, including a rapid heart rate over 150 bpm. I ask questions to narrow down the problem and determine it is tachycardia secondary to CAD. We breeze through her history—no recent illnesses or respiratory concerns. She is in over-all in good health. I place an IV in her arm as my partner applies the monitor electrodes. I run a strip of her tachycardia and can see it is significant. I radio Medical for any immediate treatment, and we get her ready to go. As I put on her coat, she asks her granddaughter to go upstairs for her own coat and hat.

With the girl out of range, the woman leans in and says quietly, "Listen, I'm all that girl has. Her parents died, and I'm all she got in this world. I need your help to make sure I can get back home with her soon. Certainly, you can understand?"

"Yes, I promise we will take good care of you and get you back home as soon as possible."

I pulled her coat over her shoulders and seat her comfortably on the stretcher. Her granddaughter glides down the stairs and we escort her to grumbling ambulance. She looks scared, and I assure her everything will be ok.

Back in the box next to grandma, I ask how she is, and she reaches for my hand.

"I'm short of breath…nothing can happen…" she whispers.

We bring her into the ER with her granddaughter at her side. I pull the doctor over and tell him my concerns, not only her rhythm but what she said to me. She believed this was the end and was concerned for her granddaughter's care.

The doctor stops shuffling his papers and looks at me like I'm being a superstitious or dramatic. "Tachycardia. We will take care of it."

His response doesn't bring me relief or convince me the treatments would be conclusive. But I had to get back in service. I ask if the granddaughter can stay with her with grandma, and the nurse says she will try to keep her there. We call back in service and return to our base station, only to run more calls.

07:00. 18 September 1991. A couple hours later we get a call for the same address for cardiac arrest. Another crew went first, so we head over to back them up. The grandmother had been treated quickly and discharged home before she went into cardiac arrest. I couldn't believe they sent her home so quickly—despite my warnings.

In the ER, I catch a glimpse of the granddaughter, but I don't have a chance to talk to her. This must be so difficult for her to witness. It would be the start of a long, lonely journey for her. I could not believe the stupidity of it all. This could have been prevented.

I am off shift by 08:00. I need to talk with my Medical Control Physician about this. I drive back down to the hospital from my base station still in uniform and head straight to his secretary's desk.

"The doctor is in but has a busy schedule today," she tells me. "Could you schedule another day?"

"It is important," I bellow. He hears me from his office and comes out.

"Come on in and tell me what is on your mind," he says.

I quickly explained the call, the situation with her granddaughter, the transition of care, lack of concern, and of course the outcome. He already knows the story but allows me to vent.

"I'm sorry, we really screwed up. Appears we made a mistake sending her home."

"A mistake? What's going to happen to that kid? I promised her grandmother everything would be okay; I said she would be taken care of. I told that doc last night and he didn't listen. I can't believe this." I wasn't pleased; in fact, I was livid with that attending doctor and this system.

"I know. I'm sorry."

I knew the chief medical control doctor would do everything he could to correct those who failed to do their job properly and have services follow-up with the granddaughter so she would be cared for. There was simply nothing else that could be done about the loss.

I drive back by the house and pull over. Just hours ago, a grandmother cared for her last family member there, and now this catastrophe destroyed what they had in a matter of hours. I should have stayed at the hospital. I had sensed that doctor was not going to do everything he could to take care of her. No, I knew she was going to be "processed" in the hospital machine of catch and release: "Please sign here on the line for billing at the bottom. Thank You."

They were not my family, but they might as well have been. That woman and child had a spirit and innocence that was common among many residents here, just good people. I thought of that look in her eyes when she asked me for help. It remains with me today. That connection was the reason I did this job and knew I had to do better. I wasn't there just to treat and transport; I was also there for support and to advocate for those who couldn't advocate for themselves.

I thought of my brother and family a lot after that call. I could not count the times I had advocated for my brother at the hospital. Just as with my brother who could not speak because of his disability, patients often need someone to speak for them, to get them the specific care they need. I learned from this experience that I had to be advocate more for those in need. Still, I couldn't help feeling sick about that kid now being alone. I wondered if I could help. What could I do? I was a cash broke ambulance driver. If I even tried to help, I would probably just scare the poor kid. All I could do was hope social services would do their job well.

21:20. 10 September 1993. My partner and I are idling next to the Chinese restaurant on Venture and Sumner when we hear the loud cracks from behind us. Coming up fast, I see a young man sprinting toward us as he passes beneath each dim yellow streetlight. His long coat flares out behind him as he lunges forward, winded. He runs up to the passenger side where I'm sitting.

He barks out between gasping breaths, "They're trying to kill me—you gotta help me."

"Jump in the back. We're getting out of here," I say.

I can see he is limping. He yanks open the side door and throws himself on the floor. We take off with the side door still open.

"Go, go!" I shout.

We drive across the street into a back parking lot of a video rental shop. I jump in the back, close the side door behind me, and turn on the dim cabin lights, knowing the hunters weren't far behind. I help him on the stretcher and remove his dark trench coat. It is pierced by a few bullet holes that must have missed him but hit the coat flaring out like a cape as he ran. A quick assessment shows he has one bullet in the back of his upper calf. He thinks he was hit in the shoulder, but the bullet must have been caught by the layers of his sweatshirt and coat. Overall, he is ok so it is time to go.

"We're all set," I say to my partner. "You can go. I'll work en route." Handling this kind of incident takes some strategy and tactfulness to get cooperation.

There is not much support you can provide for teens who think they're invincible. I can see his facial expression is fixed with disdain. His eyes have that hateful stare. He's on the wrong path, out late raising hell, gets' shot, and needs a quick ride to the ER. Once patched up he'll be back out here in a week. At times I would say a few brotherly words, "What the hell are doing out here getting filled with holes? You're smarter than that."

"Nothing, none of your f--ing business, and what do you know about me?"

"Look, we could've taken off, and you would be swiss cheese back there. I don't have to get shot for you. I just saved your ass so I'm telling you: I know you're worth more than plot in the ground. We've been picking you guys up a lot lately, so you're all not going on to bigger and better things. You want nice things in life, you have to start with life first," I say.

"Life first, easy for you to say."

"Hey, I started with less than you. I was living on oatmeal after school and driving a tow truck for five bucks an hour."

"Why don't you fix my leg?" he grumbles.

"God first. Do some good, and maybe some good will come of it."

"You sound like my aunt."

"Maybe you should listen to your aunt. I could be pulling a sheet over your head right now back on the street. Don't make me do that, okay?" It's the way I say it; like I'm an older brother who cares. My partner says we're not the same 'color' so I'm wasting my breath. I disagree. The kid knows I'm the one out here risking my neck for him and that matters.

The message seems to slowly submerge in, maybe.

I think, these wayward kids. Once in a blue moon, I hear about a kid we helped who went on to get a job, or go back to school. For the street medic, it is the opportunity to connect that has real impact. He's bleeding and I can't hide it so he sees the result. Bleeding in the back of ambulance, getting bandaged up after being shot may not seem an ideal time for counseling, *but the seriousness of the moment lends itself to an open mind.* He didn't listen before and he's not going to listen later. At this painful moment the kid just might listen. Combine that moment along with the singular interactions with the cop, teacher, town merchant, businessperson next door, pastor or reverend, even the hospital staff at times—and maybe we can heal more than a gunshot wound.

02:36. 10 August 1992. We are posted at the dry clean laundry at the south end of town. We can see in all directions including a mile or two down the dual-lane main drag. It is a quiet night, not one single car or person on the road.

We dose off listening to the police scanner. There is a commotion on the city channel after midnight—something about a domestic dispute on the east side, male suspect with a handgun. The state PD is in pursuit, down 291 west and up I-91 south at high speed. The chase turns onto Long Hill and is heading up Sumner. I can see the lights of his car coming toward us at high speed and police cruisers behind, bright blues blazing. His car screeches to a stop at the intersection right in front of us. We roll forward to get closer and see what is going on. I can see he is thinking. I can see his head tip back. Then a piercing explosion and a bright yellow flame flashes. It is enough to tell us he stuck a handgun to the roof of his mouth and pulled the trigger.

It appears the threat is over, and maybe we can help. We drive up to the car with the lights on, park, walk up to the window and check him. His brains were blown out on the ceiling of the car, and while some trapped air flowed out of his mouth in a mist, he is clearly dead with injury incompatible to life. I put my scope to his chest through the window. I hear no heart or lung sounds.

At that moment, three police cruisers pull up and walk over.

"He's dead," says one of the three uniformed men.

"Any vitals?" asks another.

"No. What happened?" I ask.

No response. The police begin their investigation of the car and take pictures of the scene.

This is another experience I did not wish to include, but I feel I must to provide context, so you can understand the big picture. While we couldn't do anything for this guy or his family, it leaves the medic frustrated and thinking, *Okay, what the hell can I do?* That feeling is often a social and mental pitfall for first responders who are trying to do good but come up empty. The importance of these horror stories is to know that while they can be discouraging, they can also be motivating for some of us stubborn types who will not accept defeat.

Sure, I can't help the guy who blows his head off in front of me, but I refuse to accept his hopeless attitude. When we medics respond to your home and stride in with a positive attitude, it's not only in the face of your challenges. We're fighting the good fight against all odds from the traffic, wayward people, lawyers, weather, bullets, and loss of life. When you're out here, it's not just about the flesh and blood. You can see that violence emanates from the accusations, lies, stealing, cheating—from sins. When violence rules, the spirit of an entire community is assaulted, and that damage is far more invasive than clips in the news can depict. All this is not an accident but by design. This is not a crazy theory but real, observable actions with consequences that are documented in a specific time and place. The fact that most people do not even believe Satan exists is his greatest trick of all.

05:52. 25 November 1992. We have just cleared a scene on a side street when I hear a woman screaming across the street, maybe thirty feet away. I see a large man behind her with his left arm wrapped around her and lifting her off the ground. He is swinging his right arm, and it looks as like he is punching her in the thigh. My partner looks for a break in the traffic to get across, and we turn on our emergency lights. I hit the siren and keep punching the ambulance forward, but the heavy traffic won't yield. I see the man drag her around the side of the building to get her out of sight. We have to push across, so I kick the gas pedal hard straight at them.

We cut through the traffic and push over the walkway at him. The woman is now free and stumbling toward us, clearly injured. The attacker starts across the parking lot, and I jump out with my trusty metal thermos to clock him with. He is walking casually, as if nothing is wrong. He is going through what looks like a purse and laughs as I yell for him to stop. He bolts, throws the purse back over his head, and pulls off his jacket, but I can see him running down the next side street. My partner calls to me that the woman has been stabbed. I run back to assist. The knife wound in her thigh is deep and spurting blood—and she has already lost a lot. We apply pressure to control the bleeding but it isn't working. Her skin is pale, and she appears to be in shock.

In the back of the bus, we find her pulses bounding and B/P dropping as we start an IV and apply military anti shock trousers (MAST). It seems to stop the bleed, and we race her downtown to the trauma room. I don't know if she will make it, but she is strong. There is no doubt we were exactly where we needed to be.

I thought about it and wondered, *what if we were there a couple minutes earlier?* Maybe we could have seen his approach and stopped the attack before the stabbing. Then again, what if we were a couple minutes later, held on that prior scene; she would almost certainly be dead.

A short time later we were given Meritorious Awards for our extraor-dinary personal action" in saving this young woman's life. I didn't care about or want the award or the press meeting at the college, but I felt it would be an insult not to attend. The local news was there and gave each of us a brief interview. I said on camera that we did what most people would do with our training. That was not true. Most people would not do what we did. The college did not train me to charge and chase a violent attacker armed while he was butchering a person, risking my life. I didn't act out of a sense of duty because I believed then as now that the city could care less about me. I was not intentionally lying but evading a truth that no one would believe. If I said I was driven to save this stranger by *my belief that the Holy Spirit has me on a mission against evil,* then an ambulance crew would probably be there for me with restraints. Nor am I sure that such a statement would characterize me accurately.

I'm not a devout Christian, although I strive to be. I am not that trusting in anything that man has his hands on. But I am passionately faithful that there is a higher power, God. I believe moral deeds or "faith based works" have serious purpose and meaning to all faiths. I respect all the major faiths in this regard, and we all share this common value. It is not enough to be good in your heart, you must walk the line. I believe in the actual person, Jesus Christ, and that his good works are some of the greatest on record. However, all of this still does not explain this high-risk action or a career of risky work and exhausting efforts.

There are people who would argue that I would have performed the same in that situation even if I were an atheist due to my American pub-lic school values. They would say that my upbringing as a brain washed American kid, indoctrinated with the secular morals, ethics, and values of working class America is the reason for all my outstanding actions, deeds, dedication, and loyalty. I say that is insulting bullshit. If I'm so ethically trained, why is it that I would have smashed the assailant's skull with my steel thermos had he not let his victim loose. I made my decision as I do many times each run of each shift. I apologize for nothing and work for only one. I know exactly what I'm doing and who I'm doing it for.

Seconds mattered here, so if I even hesitated seconds for police, the young woman could be dead. Therefore, in this instance, religion, faith, and spirituality did matter.

I can attest in this life we are truly in daily battles to win a war, good versus evil. You must pick a side no matter what your religious faith, and you must actively fight for your cause. This is not about joining a religion or group identity. This is about who I am and who we strive to be as individuals. In part, this book is about taking responsibility and being accountable for my self-assigned purpose and a higher authority's mission for me. I'm not looking to acquire material things in life but to be the good son to someone much higher. That is my independent decision made of my own free will. I also believe I must share that inspiration so others will fight with me or we all lose the war.

Revelation 21:7. "He who overcomes shall inherit all things, and I will be his God and he shall be My son."

MATTERS OF THE MIND:
PSYCHIATRIC CARE IN EMS

We have made clear strides in pre-hospital EMS to care for our patients who suffer from mental illnesses over the past years; however, each year becomes tougher than the last due to dwindling funds, waning government and community support, and irresponsible health care corporations. This results in reduced staffing and the closure of psychiatric services and facilities. Make no mistake, this has been a tragedy for many patients, families, and communities.

I find it interesting that the people who advocated for the scientific movement that ushered in private psychiatric institutions and care are the same ones who abandoned public and Christian hospitals and churches. Many run by nuns and priests who had cared for the mentally ill for over 150 years in the U.S. and centuries longer in Europe—ultimately forcing many such institutions to close. So, with all these marvelous medical advancements over recent years what is left? Nothing that I can see, unless it is profitable. That's a real problem when you have a patient in the ambulance who needs help and there's nowhere to go.

In the United States between the 1860's and 1920's hospitals transformed into industrial care centers of science and technology. Many hospitals in Massachusetts privatized in the 1980's and 1990's. Since then, they have slowly relieved themselves of unprofitable programs such as those for the mentally ill, handicapped, disabled, and post-acute care. But the charitable, spiritual institutions and public hospitals have disproportionately provided care for psychiatric and those services over all these years. To me, this alone is proof that the private industrial machine and big corporate pharma is not genuinely interested in patient care—only profits. It isn't a coincidence that many big private hospitals have relabeled psychiatric care programs as "behavioral health" programs, maybe because that sounds like it's the public's problem, rather than not a mandatory program deserving of funds.

I have increasingly empathized with the mentally ill over my career as I've seen them suffer more than any population. What the public and our government fail to recognize (although they *say* they do with words but never with funding) is that this demographic crosses all lines: age, race, ethnicity, gender, income, marital status, educational, and employment. I've taken care of wealthy professionals in psychiatric crisis. Families and friends often appear shocked when they learn people they are close to are affected; it doesn't fit with their stereotype of who suffers from such disorders. Despite improvements, we need the skilled facilities (as in adequately staffed and with all aspects of care) to transfer care over to.

30 October 1998. I have to transfer a ten-year-old female to a psychiatric care center for crisis. I receive the report that the child has a history of physical and mental abuse from a single parent. The transferring nurse has me read the patient's chart as part of the mandatory report; this helps me understand her concerns with transporting the child such a distance and without any family or friends. The history and report are horrible. It makes me physically nauseas. I meet the child who seems frail and frightened, cowering in her hospital cot. Being familiar with the psychiatric facility we are transporting her to, I think it's important to talk with the transferring physician.

"I've met this ten-year-old child for transport to this facility. I'm not sure you're familiar so I was hoping to discuss this transfer."

"Sure, what's the matter?"

"Well, it's is a very large, older facility, and the units are now combined. There is no division by age or gender. Some of the patients on the floor, are, well, large adults, aggressive, even violent. I don't think this is the best place for a child with PTSD."

"I see. Well, I might agree, but there are no beds available anywhere else. So, for tonight I think it's best just to get her a bed and some medicine. Maybe they can make new arrangements once her three days are completed," he says hopefully.

"I understand. Could you consider a medical bed here, maybe even the ER for a day until you can find a child unit? I have to be blunt, sir, this place is like a prison. Imagine a dim lighted prison with people screaming all night. It's like hell, sir." It's the most honest image I can deliver.

"I'm very sorry. I have to use the most appropriate facility approved by her insurance."

"Oh, I see. That's it, insurance. Well, it's not appropriate. Thank you." And with that we have to transport her to this dungeon.

We arrive about 2:00 am and are guided through the labyrinth of hallways and locked metal doors to the co-ed unit. As we roll the stretcher with the pale, frightened child down the hall, the piercing screams and shouts of patients echo down the laminated corridor. My patient cups her hands over her ears, trying to shut out the noise. She squeezes her eyes shut, holding her breath and trembling in fear. I stop the stretcher and ask to talk with our dark leader from hell away from our terrified kid.

"Excuse me, nurse, is there a more appropriate unit—quiet, safe, for children, especially tormented children who suffer from abuse?"

"I am sorry," she says apathetically. "We have lost two wings and this unit is the only one of its level open at this time."

"Lost your two wings?" I could only think of an angel's wings but didn't have the guts to tell her so.

After some back and forth debate, the nurse agrees to request another facility with the manager in the morning, but for now, all she can do is take the girl to another quieter room. I know our patient will still hear all the yelling and screaming, but I have no authority here. I have to leave her where the doctor ordered. I would make a complaint in the morning. I wish her well and say that I will see about getting her in a nice, quiet place. I want to give her a hug, but that wouldn't be professional, and she would probably only pull away out of her never-ending distress.

One of the hardest moments of many in my work was leaving that little girl on that unit in that place. My heart broke. Children like this need a strong patient advocate in the large, disconnected system. Years ago, more families stayed together to provide such guidance, care, and oversight. My folks spent their adult lives advocating for my brother Doug as he was treated at multiple hospitals; they always supported and represented him for better care. The loss of psychiatric beds has become a major problem in our state and across the country from what I understand. This has a critical impact on those mentally ill who need the beds urgently.

01:00. 1 December 1995. As we enter the apartment, I pause. Something is off. The vibe isn't right. The dim lighting emanates from one small yellow bulb in a shaded lamp next to the bed. The massive American flag on the wall catches my eye—it's out of the ordinary, especially with the crossed swords on it. My eyes round the darkened room noting all the rifles and Vietnam memorabilia hanging on the walls and come to rest on the lone man sitting back, propped on the bed against the wall. He has a bandana around his head. His hair is long, and he has a thick dark beard. Both his hands are down by his side, and he looks mentally and emotionally exhausted.

"Hello Sir, did you call for us?"

"No, I guess the psychiatric service did," he says without much concern.

I look over at my partner, and he nods in confirmation; it was him who took the call from dispatch.

"OK, well, are you having a tough time? Can we help you?" I offer.

I walk around his bed to the far side. I'm looking at him and notice a gleam of silver on the wooden nightstand next to his bed. I can see that gleam is light reflecting off the bullet cylinder of a large caliber revolver lying flat, within his reach. Next to that is a pack of cigarettes and an ashtray.

I suddenly realize, as all EMT's do sooner or later, that I've walked into a serious problem, one that could be painful and deadly. I have no idea if the police are on their way because they don't always come to these calls. It depends on what the caller says—the urgency, the risk. If the psych service called, then they probably mentioned a potential for harm but then again, they might not know.

I quickly consider my options and decide I should befriend this guy with honesty and integrity. If I don't or I try to walk out, I may be seen as another enemy. Then again, no matter what I say or do, listening always helps. He's obviously depressed, and the gun isn't just for show. Does he have a plan?

"Has the service you spoke with offered any help? How can we help? What can we do?"

"No, they don't know. Do you?" he says. His speech is drawn, and I sense anger, maybe alcohol or drugs on board.

"We can help. Can we make some calls and get you someone you want to see?"

No response. The room is silent as he stares at me with lids half closed.

I look around for a telephone but don't see one. I inch forward to close the distance in case he reaches for the gun. I'm not fearless nor foolish, but I'm not going have my head blown off or watch him blow off his. I glance at my partner and he sees the gun too; he looks as scared as me. We both have dealt with plenty of firearms at scenes, but it is different when you sense a person is serious about using it.

"I'm going to get the stretcher, ok, sir?" my partner says. I'm guessing he's also stepping out to call the cops. "I'll be back in a couple; we'll take you wherever you want." And he softly steps out the door.

"I want to help you," I say.

"Do you…really?"

"Yes," I say clearly and with conviction. "I don't have to be here. I can go drive a truck, but I care, I seriously care. If you don't trust those people, trust me. I'll drive you myself out to Boston in my own car if that's where you want to go."

He slowly sat up on the bed, stabilizing himself. He looks around, down at the gun just behind him on the table, then back up at me.

We both know what he could do. I remain quiet for a few seconds. I think of what is left to say at a moment like that.

"I have faith," I say.

"In who?"

"That someone, out there… can help you help yourself."

With that he thinks to himself for what seems like several minutes. I feel the tension and think in the first seconds that he is going to go for the gun, maybe not for me, but to end his pain. Minutes go by, and I can hear him thinking, see his head tremoring side to side. Then, I see tears, and he lets out a big sigh.

"OK. I'll try, to have faith." And he decides to go with us to the hospital.

In the ambulance, he asks we keep mention of the gun quiet. Of course, I tell him that he should reveal that to the crisis team. I check in later, he did.

If we had handled that situation more by the book, more impersonally, with the canned diffusion statements he was familiar with; I think there would have been a different, maybe deadly outcome.

20 August 2008. Suburb of Springfield. We receive a call for a 17-year-old female who drank poison. We arrive to the small, white, ranch-style home in a sea of identical houses. An older woman is standing on the front porch screaming at the top of her lungs at this 17-year-old kid who is sobbing. I walk up to the scene and tell Mom we'll take her daughter to the ER and get her help. Mom continues to scream at our backs as the kid and I walk back to the ambulance.

Once inside, the doors slammed shut by my partner, the girl breaks down again, tears and mucous streaming down her face. I clean her face off with a soft towel and sterile water, make her comfortable upright on the stretcher with two heavy blankets covering her. No vitals or questions at first, just time. I pause and watch the clock as the seconds tick slowly by, and she does the same.

"I appreciate the seconds because they take their time," I say lightly.

She smiles in appreciation of the "dad joke." She begins to rest but starts to ramble a little on what a bad person she is, and I listen.

When she is finished I say to her, "You are not bad, never have been; you were created as good; only mistakes are made and can easily be corrected."

That one sentence has made more of a difference in such situations than any medicine I have witnessed. Such talk is recognized but not as a treatment. Carefully chosen words diverted destructive thoughts, past and present, confirmed what's most important, and avowed that we're all human with an easy path to salvation. The fact that we're a "creation" is an amazing concept, much more believable than talking about a God above, and recalls that he is in control, so no worries or fault. Medicines can be effective, and we have all seen them work chemical miracles. But we aren't purely chemical creatures, and sooner or later they fail us. Likewise, I've seen outstanding psychiatric care in the all its forms work wonders for many, but alone it is yet another crutch. We continue to hear that we must give the sciences and technology more time as they're always advancing. But to an aging EMS guy like me, the clock ran out of time for many thousands that I've taken care of. We need help and we must work together on this. These people are not simply a category of patients but our own children, our future.

PRECAUTIONS AND
CONSEQUENCES

At times, EMTs risk their lives. Some of us for noble reasons, some out of duty or commitment, some because we're just dumb. Now there are those who may argue that statistics show there are not the many deaths in our EMS role. That may be true, but it doesn't lessen the individual risk each EMT takes on when they go into the field. No heroics here, just facts. We still knowingly walk into harm's way to help others, and there are no guarantees. The physical casualties are lower than might be expected, but in my opinion it shows we're better at winning over hearts and minds to avoid death than others. But exposure to Hepatitis, HIV, a lethal virus, or mental stress (PTSD often goes undiagnosed in our field) can take its toll untallied in the statistics and unreported in the news. I was stuck with a bloody needle while struggling with a seizing child in my clinical rotation, first of a few sticks I had. There were exposures to blood, TB, dozens of diseases, despite reducing risks with better practices. We take all the precautions but the consequences are there despite them or even because of them. We take the risks to help others, often call after call, without attention or mention because we have to, in order to do the good work for all.

20 August 1992 Springfield. Abdominal gunshot wound just a few blocks from where we are posted, making a quick response time. We enter through the front door of an old Victorian house to find a woman down the hall in the kitchen. There is a handgun a few feet away from her on the table and I secure it before she does. Then I hear a groan from the bedroom to my right, and on the floor leaning against a bed is a middle aged man holding his abdomen. There is bright red blood gushing out of the wound. I look back at the crazed woman, and she runs to the corner of the kitchen and pulls out a carving knife from the drawer. She points it at me, sneering, walking around the kitchen table. "Listen, I'm not your enemy. I'm not a cop. I'm a medic, just here to help, and I'm leaving soon." I say.

"You think I shot him!" she shouts out.

"No…I'm with you. I know nothing." I pause. I don't want to talk myself in circles, and she still has the knife. "Can I stop his bleeding?" I say matter of fact, pause again, and it's quiet. I count the seconds as they go by. Out of the corner of my eye I see my partner hanging back at the front door waving me to back out. The woman looks like she could kill me, maybe even wants to.

"If he dies you could be in more trouble…and I don't want that," I say quietly, like a caring brother talking to his hurt sister. I say it seriously, and it kind of surprises me that I mean it.

"Go," she says lifting her head toward his doorway.

I apply a trauma dressing to his gushing abdominal wound and the exit wound out his back, but he is crashing fast in shock. Pale, eyes glazing over.

The police enter and turn to me with their backs to her in the kitchen. I quietly tell them to watch their backs as she has a knife. We get him out, and she calms down.

You know, I reflected on it after the call. Was this a domestic dispute? Was she defending herself after abuse, or was she the abuser? Maybe she was mentally ill. I did hundreds of these calls over the years. It's not my business, and it doesn't matter when I'm performing my job—or does it? Should it?

How can I treat a patient correctly if I'm not allowed to know what I'm treating? Our protocols allow us to gain information and treat by interacting. The way we interact depends on what we know and our motivation to use that information to help. Either that motivation is a higher calling to improve the health and lives of people, even save lives at times, or it's a lowly job with a deficient function like that of a street sweeper. That depends first on the practitioner but also on local authorities, government, and communities themselves and how they choose to see us and interact with us.

Here I have to give the local government credit regarding the use of private EMS as public safety servants. It's a brilliant and cunning concept. Take a couple loyal people who want to make a difference and put them in a truck in the center of your city to respond to anyone who dials the three little numbers everyone knows. Even better, post them strategically in high need neighborhoods on street corners like the five-cent beat cop of the 1930's. Yes, kind of a crisis crew that can handle any emergency, title us EMT's, Paramedics, sounds important.

Cities intentionally choose relieve themselves of this responsibility. Our city dumped this responsibility they once partnered with the fire department back in the 1970's. They hired a private third-party company and gave the whole headache to them, the suckers who can't sue the city (effectively) when they're assaulted or break their backs. Private EMTs have little recourse for labor disputes and sometimes are made completely responsible when they incur injuries. By responsible I mean I have seen injured EMTs continue to suffer problems long after the private company they worked for went out of business. The employee's only recourse is to file a lawsuit with the city, which is protected against legal liability by the contracted company's insurance, perhaps now unreachable. Some of the legitimate cases wind up on permanent disability.

13 June 1997 Springfield. I'm working the road with a brand new, basic EMT one evening. We are driving north to the hospital and cross a major intersection. Behind the convenience store on the corner store is a punk sniper hidden in the alleyway. Suddenly, the passenger window explodes. Boom! The glass shatters all over my partner, flying across and raining down on me, too. Shocked, I lose control and swerve over the median into oncoming traffic. I cut the wheel, bringing us back over to our side and brake to the curb.

"Hey!" I say looking over at my EMT. He's just a kid. "Are you OK?"

For a second I think he has been shot in the head. He's staring straight out the windshield. His chest and lap are covered in a layer of broken glass.

"Hey, are you OK? Talk to me."

"Yes, I'm fine," he says with uncertainty.

"Let me see your face…let's check…" I scan his head and upper torso, his shoulder. "You look ok…that was a bullet…those…" I am overwhelmed by a surge of anger. It takes me over. "They shot us…an ambulance. You little bastards! I'm gonna kill this piece of shit."

I throw the shifter in drive and punch it forward taking the next side street on the right to circle around behind the punk who I figure must be fleeing the scene. I figure he must have run back through the alley and in backyards between houses. I think it must have been a 22 gauge at most, and I can just run him over or catch him and pound the shit out of him.

As we race down the side street with the gas pinned, I hear the kid next to me making a long humming noise. I look over and he is sheet white.

"What's the matter, are you still okay?"

"Yeah, but can we just stop?"

"No, this guy's going to pay."

We round the corner about a football field away from where the shot came from. I stop, turn the lights off, and shut the engine to listen. We peer into the dark backyards but see no movement. I realize the shooter could have jumped a fence to one the smaller side streets. I fire the rig up and keep searching, waiting, listening. I can hear my own breathing and big sighs from my kid partner. He heaves a long breath out, and I sense his apprehension.

"Can we stop? This guy has a gun, and I don't want to get shot. Maybe we should just call the cops," he says. It's the sensible thing to do.

"The cops aren't going do shit." I replied.

The look on his face says it all, *I'm done, let's go home.*

I'm still angered, but I see his point. He is being the intelligent adult here, and I need to shape up and take responsibility to get us to a safe place and some assistance. I reverse up the whole length of the side street crowded by single family homes. I call dispatch on our limited cell phone of the time and explain. When an officer arrives, he inspects the now missing window and the cab floor for a bullet. He concurs it was either a small caliber or even an air gun but seems to find it harmless fun.

"We get cabs shot all the time. Nothing we can do."

"Should we write a report?" I ask.

"Nah, don't waste your time," he says with the dismissive wave of the hand.

Just great, I think. We could have been plugged in the head. Small caliber or not, the gunman was aiming to hurt us, not pop the tire. And what does he mean they 'get cabs shot all the time?' So, is it open season on cabs and ambulances? What if he shot a police cruiser? Would that be waved off with a hand? I know it wouldn't be. I know it and have to face it; politically, we are just trash-men to the city—no better, no worse. It is one reason these cities lose so many good EMT's, their worth is obvious, and they leave the job.

I bring the kid back to our base station and clean him up. Only a couple tiny scratches. I feel bad this is his introduction to EMS. He was a young kid, about nineteen, a good kid.

He came to my office a couple days later and resigned. I don't blame him at all; he deserved better and this town didn't deserve him. I went back to that shooter location behind the convenience store several evenings over the next week hoping to find something or bump into someone looking guilty. Nothing there, just a dirty alley.

As a civilian medic in America, one must take all insults and assaults as part of the job and understand that the assailants are exempt…somehow.

Besides the daily insults, medics endure some minor assaults. I have: been punched, kicked, thrown, checked, stabbed at, shot at, spit at, had objects thrown at, bled on, puked on… you get the picture. It's not as bad as in some countries but we could use extra help, hold the bricks.

16 August 1994 Springfield. 911 call for an unknown in the College Street section of town at a derelict, abandoned Victorian home. We pull up quietly with the emergency lights off. I ask my partner to kill the engine, but he's hot and wants the A/C to run while I check out the complaint. We radio to confirm the address with the dispatcher but she didn't respond. So it goes.

The house is pitch black—no lights on and no cops here—great. We park so the rear doors would be close to the walkway. I get out, pause to listen for any sounds from the house, and grab my first-in bag. I walk along the tall, thick hedges lining the sidewalk. As I approached the front porch, the hedge opens a little, and someone thrusts a black handgun out leveled at my head.

"Stop," says an angry, male voice from behind the hedge.

I can't see anyone, just the muzzle of the gun a couple feet from my face.

"Move and I'll blow your fuckin' head off. What are you doing here, in my neighborhood?" he says.

"We got a call for someone here, unknown problem, just here to help."

"Get out of here."

"OK."

I turned slowly, ready to duck or run—as if I could outrun a gunshot so close, but what choice did I have? I walk steadily back to the ambulance without looking back; I think he may shoot me in the back. I throw my bag in the side door and jump up front.

"Drive. Get out of here. Now."

My partner speeds off and I call dispatch. I tell her what happened and that we are leaving the scene. She says we should go back—without police—but I refuse.

The dispatcher probably thought I was exaggerating. Maybe it was just a bluff, a prank. Home of Smith and Wesson after all. We didn't even bother reporting it. Some days, it was like being in a circus: we were just another act.

Some see a paramedic as that unknown, not a member of any reputable group, an expendable person who takes the job knowing the risks because they themselves are worth risking. Another physician told me in EMS, "The lowest bidder gets the job." He was right; what ambulance company walks into a town advertising the highest pay and benefit packages? But does everyone in the general public see it this way? Is it worth it as a career, for how long, and to what end?

A lot depends on place and time and most importantly who you work for. In the 1980's in a working-class community, we were often treated with a modicum of respect and appreciation. But after that time, in an urban setting forget it—you have no idea with who you are responding to, and you're on your own.

A couple medics I worked with wore bullet-proof vests. They claimed this helped but it may also have made them targets. We had one medic was standing aside a front door as he knocked at night on a 911 call. The response was a shotgun blast through the middle of the door. He wasn't hit. There were other close-calls when the vest seemed to do its job. However, I recall most vested medics sweating-up a storm in the heat and suffering limited mobility; hence the consequence of that protection.

14 May 1989 Springfield. His car rolled into the rear of a tractor trailer which braked on the down slope section of the highway bridge. I'm assessing the seatbelted, lone male driver who is complaining of posterior neck pain around his third cervical vertebrae. The police officer is outside the car telling me the accident appeared to be at very slow speed, maybe even 10-15 mph. I can see the shoulder belt was high and may have worked as a hangman's cord or 'low branch' by holding him immovable but not his head. Problem is he is beginning to show signs of a spinal cord injury. We immediately take stabilization of his head and neck as we apply the cervical collar in the car. Sweating profusely, he sounds nervous and short of breath with muscle weakness, and reduced sensation in his extremities with a pins and needles feel. Upon arrival at the hospital in minutes' he's developing a loss of sensation and movement in his legs and feet. Our medical control doc thinks he is becoming paralyzed.

The advertised slogans run through my mind like those on the highway billboards. Seatbelts save lives. 55- stay alive. Speed Thrills but Kills. These are true, at times. I have seen much success of the wisdom as they save thousands of lives. I have also seen patients injured by their seat belt; lulled into multicar pileups driving in herds at the heavy-eyed 55, and crushed at slow somnolent speeds. The turtle cannot outrun the tractor, and they are both slow. Ever talk with a tired old medic and he seems to doubt safety advice? Maybe he learned everything is unsafe in the hands of an idiot. Recall what we learned as kids: it is not just what you do, but how, when, where and why. Wearing a seatbelt is useless if everyone is driving selfishly, reckless, texting, talking, distracted, unfocused, uncaring. So do not wear one to 'be safe.' To be really safe do not drive on that road at that time with those people…period. Listen to the crippled and the dead. Lessons learned.

"You're safer to wear a bullet proof vest." experts say. Not if they want to shoot you in the head. Vests are hot, bulky and restrictive, making defense and patient care difficult. Precautions can have consequences.

"We must all wear masks to end the spread of disease." Masks are good. Yes, we got that memo 24/7 this year and every year past. In EMS we are exposed going into every house, nursing home, hospital, jail, facility, and public place more than anyone. We live in masks, gowns and gloves. *Protective gear is good.* Has forcing people to wear them every second saved everyone? No, it has both failed and succeeded. Like all health care personnel, I recently had an eighty-something year old patient who would not keep his mask on. He was just diagnosed with COVID in the ER. He would pull it down to talk to us and we would politely ask him to pull it back up, about once every minute. His elderly buddy rolled-up in a wheelchair and pulled his mask down to tell our patient to pull his up. Because they can't hear each other they get closer together, talk louder and cough more.

Despite wearing more personal protective equipment (PPE) than most, EMS personnel working in infected areas have become sick. Seems frequency of exposure increases risk of illness regardless. But data has proven the general public have gotten sick without ever leaving their homes. I have seen the most cautious get sick despite all precautions. Our communities have done a great job which is all we can ask for. Communication and supportive interaction with our patients is one of the most important treatments we have and that has been sacrificed at times; which is a direct consequence that should not be ignored.

18 July 1993 Springfield. I had a medic partner who carried his pistol on the job despite regulations and my advice that if I saw him carry he could find himself jobless. I have few issues with guns, mostly in the hands of criminals, the mentally ill and medics. We arrived downtown at night on the scene of a shooting with no police or knowledge of the gunman. I walked up the three flights in the bullet-riddled, dimly-lit stairwell of the brick apartment building. Finding the young guy shot in the heel of his foot in a apartment, I treated and bandaged his wound. Soon, the police arrived and asked me if I felt safe up there not knowing the whereabouts of the gunman. I pointed to all the random missed shots and the fact the shooter could only hit his victim's heel. As we moved the patient downstairs to the ambulance outside, we stepped over a pistol magazine on the stairs, chaulked-off and taped-off by police as "evidence." I thought, I didn't see that walking up. In the ambulance my partner advised me the loaded magazine was in fact his and had fallen out of his pocket. I advised he tell the police the truth before he ruined their case. That is the typical consequence of a handgun carried in civilian EMS.

7 June 1991 Springfield. An old time police officer carried the classic silver six shooter with pearl grips. It matched his silver hair. We were at a house for a call for help by a disturbed person. I went to enter a room where a patient was waiting for us but the senior officer pulled me back and stepped in first with his shiny gun drawn, pointed up. As we entered the man awaited seated at his desk with his own gun in hand. The officer did not point his gun at the man. He only had to show his gun to end the threat. Really, he was showing the man why it was a bad idea. Perhaps it is like the cold war. Maybe guns are better ready to shoot than being shot.

THE RESIDUAL OF
THE ROTTEN

When you're trying to answer the question, "Do spirit and religion matter in the battle between life and death?" the Satanic cannot be ignored as they assert the opposite. I find it frustrating: I don't know if we can always help them, but it's critical to try. I will not refer to Satanists as a faith because they obviously lack any. Working with all the faiths, atheists, and agnostics to provide comfort is difficult enough. But when you have a group that not only denies mainstream morality but promotes the opposite values to the spiritual and soulful—advocating the destruction of spirituality while *promoting death and suffering*—it is almost an impossible situation. This is a situation that medics have to deal with, along with: other practitioners, psychiatrists, families, communities, religious organizations, humanity, and finally God himself. We see the worst of it in the form of homicide, torture, self-inflicted torture and suffering, suicides, attempted suicides, but *most elusive is the collateral chaos and destruction.* Is this a symptom of faithlessness or a psychiatric problem? I think it can be both. But the cause of this darkness and confusion, however debatable and deniable to some, is Satan himself.

20 October 2003. We arrive on the scene of a ground level apartment. Police officers pace outside, looking somewhat perplexed. Inside, the reason for their perplexity becomes apparent. There, suspended from the ceiling by a rope noose around her neck is the body of a young woman hanging before a three-foot symbol of the satanic star of Baphomet (Satan).

Her body is limp, faced towards the symbol, lifeless, *livor mortis* in color, destroyed in a manner that I am always shocked to see.

This type of scene, unfortunately, it is not my first time to see a suicide in this manner and in front of this symbol. The blatant display of satanic symbolism shoved in my face on the grotesque scene of a young life taken is an assault. The meaning here is that this person is sacrificed to Satan. On two other hanging cases I had like this, one before and one after, each victim was kneeling, as if to bow down to Satan or to mock a genuinely religious person honoring the Lord.

I have to walk outside.

A few people are standing around on the sidewalk.

"Crazy kids, must be drugs, eh?" one guy says, laughing nervously.

Christ, why are they not angry? Who could possibly say this is an acceptable way to die? There are people who are malleable enough to think that this is really not a sacrifice but a "wayward child" victim, lumped in with the misguided, confused, mentally ill, or chemically imbalanced category. It infuriates me because I've heard these small groups argue that practicing rituals under this legal organization, if you can call it that, is their right. Well, here is the result of that practice. And for those who say symbolism doesn't mean anything, you know, it's just drawing, a patch, a tattoo—well, here there was an innocent human life sacrificed to that symbol.

My role in this tragedy is to definitively determine that she is in fact dead for the police to continue their investigation. I quickly go through my assessment for signs of life and document my findings in detail for my report.

It looks like she had been dead for some hours so that was conclusive. We clear out as soon as possible.

We have to speak briefly with the closest family member out of concern for their wellness, but that doesn't go well either. They are understandably angry and grieving. We offer our assistance or a ride to psychiatric counseling, but he refuses both.

"You don't give a shit. Get out of here!"

I note we are only trying to help. Ironically, I want to offer the option of access to religious services but found myself hesitant to ask about their religious inclination under the circumstances. Suppose I asked the question like so, "I know you're grieving at this time, and I would like to offer some relief. I have to ask, if you are religious or have someone in mind who could comfort you at this time, could we help you get in touch with them?" Sounds pathetic, and I imagine that maybe this person is satanic too, and my suggestion will aggravate them more. I am truly at a loss. It is my job to help people, but in these situations, however rare, it is impossible.

We see this "sacrifice" resonate through the entire community. The victim's family, friends, and many people hear this news and are hurt and saddened because they too; have been assaulted. This is how the "residual of the rotten" came to my mind, witnessing this intentional destruction of spirit spread.

12 July 1991. York Street Jail, Springfield. We respond to the York Street Jail ("The Big House"), the archaic brick and steel bar fortress looming above us downtown by the river on West Columbus Street. Built in 1887, the building alone gave one pause, surrounded by a flint-black iron fence. We went in through the front "sally port" box, then the Reception Hall, and onto the open grass main yard outside where a man lay unconscious and unresponsive. A group of inmates and security guards surround the man who the head guard tells me simply "dropped." He adds that he thinks the patient uses intravenous drugs. As I assess, that is immediately apparent by the needle marks (coined "track marks" in our day) on both arms, both legs, and at every palpable vein visible. We support his breathing with supplemental oxygen and assist with bag valve ventilations. While my medic partner is taking vitals and monitoring his cardiac function, I search for a vein with little success, except for his long saphenous vein on the inside of his right thigh. I canalize this with ease, and we push the naloxone slowly so as not to wake him too abruptly. Suddenly waking a patient, who is heavily sedated by opiate drugs can backfire with rapid withdrawal symptoms as well as the Naloxone's dozen side effects.

"John" awakens and requests to leave this "hell hole," which is no surprise. I don't know what he did to end up here, but it doesn't seem that anything less than the worst crimes should warrant time in this dungeon. Hell, I feel just as bad for the sheriffs who have to work here. We load him into the ambulance and transport him to the hospital quietly. He's stable now, and the guard comes along for the ride. The patient's boney frame has little flesh on it, maybe weighing just over 100 lbs. As we bounce along down the road,

John is sweating, shaking, vomiting, and getting very nervous. Some of this is the drugs or whatever he was injecting, but some is from his experiences inside the prison.

"We're bunked on top of each other like sardines. The temp is like a hundred at night, the stench is insane. This guy is beating the crap out of me for the cash I owe him for this shit [heroine]. I gotta end this," John says.

"Okay, let's get you some help."

"What, shrinks?" He means psychiatric doctors. "What are they gonna do? They're gonna try to brainwash me that this is temporary. It's never ending. Most of my family is fucked up or dead, my friends are dead..."

John rambled on about an apartment he lost, family disappointments, one thing after another. He mumbled accusations, guilt, shame. There seemed to be a pattern. I do not judge what anyone is responsible or accountable for in life. There are other people whose job it is to do that. Once again, there is another adversary that judges, accuses, condemns, and punishes on a huge scale. My job is to treat, transport, and be there when needed.

The York Street Jail, a relic of a structure, was overcrowded. Designed to hold 256 inmates, it was reported to have more than 700 by the 1980's. This building was literally falling to pieces when I was going there for the sick and injured. The cells were six feet x eight feet wide with nine foot masonry walls. The men's cell block facing West Columbus was four floors tall with caged catwalks, smelled of damp masonry, peeling lead paint, mold, and sweat. It was such a dangerous situation that the Sheriff commandeered the National Guard armory in 1990 to house prisoners. He had to use an obscure 17th century law that allowed him the power to do that. The jail was closed but that took too many years.

During the 1980's into the 1990's, I had done a number of responses there for all sorts of problems including a fire. It is hard to describe the ancient, open interior, iron bars, and steep stairs. Carrying out patients in a stair chair was as miserable and risky to us as the patients; there were always inmates hanging on the bars of their cells, yelling, cursing. Its history and those voices echoed inside. We're glad it was demolished. Those incarcerated wanted out and had many stories of the rotten conditions they endured inside. Hopefully corrections can do more correcting and less punishing. We don't know where to find the hope and faith in a facility like that or the modern ones of today. According to my patients one can only find it within and beyond themselves and not the place they are in.

THE PARABLE OF
THE LOST ADDICT

20 August 1991 Springfield. I leave home early in the morning feeling a bit uneasy about the twenty-four hour shift that lay ahead of me. On my last few shifts, I had been responding to repeated calls for three heroin abusers who had been using some bad stuff going around, and it's all bad.

One man, we'll call him Luther, promised me the last time I woke him up with Naloxone (Narcan) that he was going to be, "A good dad and a father," wow, two for one. He was supine on my stretcher in the bus with barely any air moving in his lungs. I pushed a third full dose of Narcan in his arm, and his vitals still didn't budge a breath or beat. Then, suddenly, without the sign of the cross, his eyelids sprang open and his pupils dilated slightly. It could take 20 minutes or more to show good signs of life, or he could awake like a bear. I find it ironic that the heroin user's pupils constrict as if to keep out the light of anything good. It's actually the dope blocking signals of the sympathetic nervous system, which supports breathing, heart rate, and blood pressure; it leaves your system vulnerable and vitals drop dangerously low. Narcan removes the blocker at the receptor so the sympathetic system can work again. Luther was suddenly very conscious and aware that he needed to battle this grip of evil—and it is evil.

"Rejoice with me Luther, you're alive and ready to begin a new day," I said.

"I promise you, man. I got two kids. I need to kick this. I'm gonna be a good dad and a father." Then he began to cry, a grown man in his thirties.

I hadn't seen Luther the rest of that shift. But I had seen the others.

Tracy was a regular too, and last shift I took her over to the methadone clinic after her last respiratory arrest in my rig. It took several doses of Narcan to make her breath, and she understood that.

The doctors at the hospital say only about one fifth will win their war against addiction after numerous battles for about a year. Tracy had been hooked for well over a year and was showing the physical signs of its torment; she was thin, weak, pale, shaking, had poor circulation and slow movements. When Tracy was over-dosed (or I say "drugged because there is no proper therapeutic dose) her pupils not only constricted—her eyes moved as if possessed.

Tracy said she would "stay around" because she liked to see me, as if these calls were for dinner and a movie. Last I saw, she was walking upright into the clinic.

"Tomorrow is supposed to be a sunny day. Maybe you can get outdoors, enjoy the day?" I offered before departing. "I'll do that, thanks." she said with a smile.

This is often the only type of advice these people would listen to and maybe hear. If I ever tried to talk about kicking their vice "grip" they would drop me like the bad habit first.

Beth was another regular. We would often pick her up from motel rooms, always left alone after her dealer had split. Beth was just a kid, maybe 18 years old with classic features that I imagined were stunning when she was healthy and happy. Last time I saw her, another ambulance crew had just wheeled her out of the motel room, blue and apneic. Driving across the parking lot, I recognized the blond locks of hair but thought she was dead.

I jumped in the back of the ambulance. The EMT at the head of the stretcher made some wise crack. I threw the bag valve mask hand ventilator (BVM) hard into his chest and barked the order.

"Bag her now," I said.

"Wow, she was something, this one, eh?" he cracked.

"Shut up and ventilate her now..." *or you're going out the door on your fuckin' face*, I thought. "Cover her with a blanket. Does she not deserve a blanket? Do it now."

I was getting louder. They started to move quicker, sensing I wanted to snap their scrawny necks like they were the drug dealer themselves. Not much better if you're contributing to the cause, I thought. What's the difference anyway between causing this or watching it as entertainment?

I had an IV line in seconds. My partner held the angio while I pushed the Narcan before I even had it taped down. I kept pushing dose after dose as we connected all the equipment, and I don't know why but it felt like I was losing a little sister or a daughter. Where were her parents and family? Watching this protracted death, again and again. It was killing me inside. Finally, some minor movements and then a giant gasp for air. Slowly she came back from the edge of death. I ran the fluids and propped her up. She was in worse shape than last time. She was covered in bruises and scratches.

At the hospital, I met with her after the staff was done. I tried asking her to get help, but she was asking for her boyfriend, whom I guessed was her supplier. We talked for a while, but the conversation always came back around that I didn't know her or understand.

"What's it matter to you?" she said. "There's a lot of people you can go help so leave me alone." With that she got off the gurney and pushed by me for someone who couldn't care less. I guessed at this point this wasn't my business, technically speaking, so I returned to service. I hadn't seen her since, but another crew said they think she left the area. I hoped and prayed she found her way home. I knew some are saved but some are lost.

If there's one thing I hate, it's the drug culture. I've seen far more suffering, death, and destruction caused by drug culture to tolerate it. The marketing bothers me the most because it's designed to change the viewer's thoughts, indoctrinate them, and sentence them to pain and suffering. When states and towns vote to legalize marijuana, maybe there are good intentions by the voters who wish to decriminalize it. But the purpose I see is to market the concept that drugs are a new way. Now, we have billboards with giant pictures of drugs, pipes, and paraphernalia that convey drug use as widely accepted. They promote drug use as a means to fulfillment and happiness. Like commercials for alcohol, these campaigns are selling more than marijuana, they're selling the idea of substance abuse as a good path to relief from our problems. But for every smile there are a thousand tears. *The ultimate cost is spirit, mind and body.*

In the 1980's and 90's we went to public schools and gave presentations on our work to help alleviate any fear of ambulances or medics. These were positive events that the teachers. parents and children enjoyed. I would go through our equipment and the ambulance to orient all to how it works and what we do to help. Someone in the class would always have a story to tell about a family member or friend who had been treated or transported. Occasionally the topic of drugs would surface and it was a good time to briefly reflect on the dangers without talking about laws or preaching. Seeing is believing and talking directly with medics off-duty improved understanding of what the community was up against. These events are still done but not as often and I hope the unity against the threat of drugs is not divided by the opposition that profits from the business.

The lost and divided

2 September 2006. Western Mass. I am called in to assist a 19-year-old woman who had a tachycardia event at a local college. She was working on campus when she became symptomatic and called 911.

After hauling up our gear to upstairs, we find her alone on the phone with her mom who lives overseas. She is grasping her chest and says she has "sudden tachycardia," which she had experienced before. She confirms to me that she had been treated with electrical therapy or "cardioverted."

She isn't speaking clearly, and in a panic, she thrusts the phone in my face. I want to quickly get to work, but now I'm on the phone with this kid's mother who wants assurance it will be OK, and I find myself promising I will take great care of her daughter. That's easy when everything seems straight forward. I end the conversation ASAP and begin assessing, getting vitals, and connecting her to the monitor.

The patient seems guarded and won't answer simple medical questions: brief history, meds, allergies, approximate time of last event. She's defensive. I am generally adept at gaining a rapport, trust, and confidence from my patients in seconds by asking questions short, quick, matter of fact questions—like a professional would but with the ease of an old family friend.

In this case it isn't working; she almost seems paranoid. Sensing this and given she is a teenager on a college campus I also have to ask the routine question regarding any substances used or ingested. My approach to asking had almost always put people at ease. Near the end of the assessment and as I am explaining treatment and destination as usual, I say, "Now I have to ask a routine question that I must ask everyone with tachycardia, just nod yes or no. Have you taken anything else that could affect you such as: coffee, caffeine, sports drinks, over the counter supplements like diet pills, cold or allergy medicines, alcohol, recreational drugs, anything at all that could affect your heart rate?"

To each of these she shakes her head no.

We quickly stair chair her down to the ambulance, and, seeing her heart rate over 200 with narrow complexes, I know I had to make a decision between electrical treatment (synchronized cardioversion) or chemical (medicating with Adenosine) to break it. She is symptomatic although somewhat stable. I try a Vagal maneuver called carotid sinus massage to no avail. To throw a wrench into the mix, I notice she has a specific complex that indicates a hard-to-treat rhythm. If I use the wrong method, her rhythm might not come back after being stopped to "reset" her hearts inherent pacemaker.

I call my medical control physician for advice. He says to do whichever one I think is right, so I opt for the medicine. I give her the Adenosine rapid IV push followed by a 10ml IV saline flush. Her heart rate suddenly stops and does not increase. It stays slow—bradycardic—followed by sinus arrest for several seconds, longer than typical after this medication. With that my own heart stops while I bolus her with fluid, thinking of next steps, and then her heart starts again. It returns to a normal sinus range.

We get her safely to the hospital and check in with a bedside report to the nurse and doctor. To add to my stress, the nurse tells me that the patient is unhappy with me because she feels targeted for racial profiling because I had asked her if she drank any alcohol. I'm completely shocked by the accusation. The nurse adds that the patient wanted to file a formal complaint. Of course, I explained the typical course of questioning I used and that the ER staff use themselves per standard operating procedures. The ER staff understands and say they will talk with the patient and try to reason with her while I complete paperwork.

I meet with the patient afterward as agreed upon with the MD. I apologize for any misunderstanding, and allow her to complain directly to me. She expressed her frustration and her perception of my assessment questions.

"You know, taking care of you with this rhythm was rather stressful for me" I say. "I wanted to make the right decision in treating you, and those questions are routine for any tachycardic patient. Those questions aren't specifically for you. I would ask anyone in the same position, whether they were young or old, male or female, regardless of race or ethnicity. It's about your heart, not you," I try to explain. "If you confirmed you were using alcohol or some substance I might have to completely change my treatment. For example, using certain substances with both sedative and stimulating cardiac affects, then I might have to reconsider what I give you as it could exacerbate your tachycardia. I had a critical decision to make, and I take that seriously. And you did have a rhythm that appeared different."

Despite this reasonable explanation, her response was rude, irrational, and inconsiderate. It was as if she was responding to a preconceived prejudice, not to me.

We do a job that is often misunderstood. Whenever you give someone a medication or treatment, anti-dysrhythmic medications, apply electrotherapy, or use invasive procedures, there's a lack of understanding as to the risk we're taking to make their lives better or to save them. We work to build more faith in medics and the EMS system. I've seen and treated every cardiac rhythm in the book more times than I can count. At times it's simple, but treating supra ventricular tachycardia can be a challenging because it can appear different from its underlying causes, especially in younger patients. If the patient doesn't or can't tell you details about why their illness happens; the typical treatment can stop the tachycardia for a worse problem. It's like following a recipe for chocolate cake, adding the wrong ingredient and ending up with brownies. OK, bad analogy.

In my career I have partnered with, carried, coddled, medicated, treated, cared for more humans of every conceivable race and gender than most people have shook hands with. All people to me. It's easy for critics to stand on the soapbox of the evening news, or social media opining on injustice; it's quite another to go out on the city streets and actually work hands-on helping people, some who resist the system based on what they hear. Division interferes with patient care. Our actions every day of helping every person was our visible battle against those who talked about differences and conflicts under the guise of unity. A community can help by resisting the divisional rhetoric of the media and politicians to take part in any community support from volunteering to just assisting the neighbor.

I worked in small cities or towns because of the communities and neighborhoods. In Springfield the neighborhoods were as diverse as the architecture of the houses. Known as the City of Homes it was not hard to see the range of architecture from Victorian mini-mansions to the single and multi-family houses. I worked as a teen painting some of these houses with my uncle. The pride of the neighborhoods was evident not only in the formal historic districts but visible on the sidestreets with neighbors of every ethnic origin conversing and working together.

I receive a call from dispatch for an elderly man complaining of "not feeling well," on the sidewalk of White Street by Sumner Avenue. As we roll up to the sidewalk I can see an elderly man, who appears in no distress, well dressed, standing attended by several bystanders. They are in front of a few storefronts that I know well as my grandfather occupied this one as the Victory Shoe shop for many years in distant past. I direct my attention to our patient but my coworker has this call so he is doing the assessment. Two men identify themselves as neighbors from around the block and hand me a paper with the patient's medical information, medicines and address written down. This is unbelievably helpful in case the patient cannot communicate given he is ill.

"He's our neighbor and we take care of our own." The stocky fifty something year old says with pride.

"Is he going to be okay?" asks the the other man. "He's always walking around this block talking sports and checking-in on others in the neighborhood."

I mention my association with the building's history we are in front of and recall sweeping this very sidewalk as a little kid. They share some quick history of the different shops that have been here over the years including an antique store that had some old black and white photographs of the city with its classic New England storefronts and trolley. Our patient hears the discussion and his interest is peaked as he begins to feel better and tell us about his memories of the town and its connection to others by rail and trolley. He even recalled remnants of the Trolley Barn in downtown and the company that once built trolley cars here in town. The patient's recollection sparked interest of all on scene who were there to help him. I find these brief on-scene chats valuable relationships that connect, however transient, past to present, history to his story. Medically sound, his faith intact, our patient said he had lost all his family but found daily support from his believers at church and his good neighbors.

SURVIVING TRAUMA

Sometimes it's hard to see the spirituality or the good in life when you are try-ing to de-escalate "spiraling-into-hell events" like intense assaults following domestic disputes. These events can be traumatic physically, psychologically, or both. I recall one example when a wife awaited her husband with a bucket of battery acid at the front door after his night of partying.

Apparently, she had drained off old battery acids into a bucket in their garage at night. When he came home in the early morning, she greeted him at the front door by throwing the bucket of acid in his face. We arrived minutes after to find him rolling around the front yard with his face burning and his eyes corroding.

Despite aggressive treatment, we couldn't relieve his physical pain. I found the abuse hard to rationalize as just another dispute and assault. The mental torment this guy was suffering from such a brutal assault by his wife was also untouchable at this time. And so it is, and you accept the things you cannot change. As far as pain medication, at that time we only had a synthetic derivative of morphine called Nubain (Nalbuphine), which did not help much for severe pain like this. I gave him the highest dose appropriate, and it didn't touch the intense pain.

When treating such pain, a medic can try to talk the patient through the pain; it is a good start but not enough. I often count down the time on the way to the hospital with the patient as a mechanism for governing their patience and creating a focal point other than the horrible thoughts they're having. Next I chronical their current treatment and the treatment they will get at the hospital to instill some confidence and hope. So, when the patient is screaming things like, "Oh my god my face is melting off!" instead of responding, "It will be ok," which we don't know, the better response is, "We're now five minutes out, and we have the IV and pain medication running for you," followed by, "I'm calling the doctors who will have the surgical team there waiting for you." It is much more promising and helps manage the mental chaos.

If that all fails, I revert to, "Have faith, and you'll get through this." Sometimes that helps people, especially people of faith, to find the strength to cope. And that is all you can provide at times.

So many domestic disputes with assaults highlight our society's mental ills. I could have one or many in a single shift. These assaults often appear more intense because they're retribution for intense pain and anguish. Guns and knives are only the popular weapons, but I've seen chemicals, poisonings, and an array of tools used from hammers to screwdrivers for starters. In one incident, the girlfriend ran her abuser down in her car, driving with him on the hood of the car for miles before running into a guardrail. Vehicles are often used as weapons.

Of course, beatings and rape are often the most offensive assaults because they are so personal and meant to inflict pain on multiple levels. While I prefer to erase such memories from my mind, I cannot ignore them. These were a fact of life as a medic, and dealing with the victims, the predators and the victims' family members. I cannot understand the implicit acceptance and lack of outrage by communities for such actions.

Most painful is seeing the victims suffer after the assaults. They become so fearful and untrusting of anyone, never mind a strange ambulance person arriving on scene. Trying to gain even a second of trust can be almost impossible. I've had to treat a woman cowering in the corner, shaking and growling like a wounded animal, lashing out at anyone who dared approach.

It took a very compassionate police officer and I about twenty minutes of defusing conversation (slow, compassionate, caring) to get her out of the corner without hurting herself or us.

To dispel the myth, I never found that every victim lost trust in only one gender, for example, female victims did not become solely fearful of men in general. In fact, I found these patients untrusting of anyone, regardless of gender; rather you gained their trust based on their perception that you were either completely trustworthy or not at all. Family members of victims are not exempt; in fact, often they are perceived as complicit in some ways by the victim. As care providers it doesn't matter what we say or do; it only matters how we make the patient feel. I was proud that when I could gain that trust and help as much as they would allow. Sometimes the connection is impossible; but usually the unspoken language of listening created a bridge.

After witnessing such situations up so close, at times it was difficult to just complete the paperwork, jump in the tech seat for the next run, and pretend to be unaffected. Often, I could avoid the "empathy trap" where you internalize your patients' trauma and thereby make yourself sick. Some experienced medics are great at being the "iceman." However, at times I did not want to get back in the ambulance, never mind submit myself to the cavalier statements from my partner *du-jour* of the day, "So hey Tom, how about those Patriots? What a game last night." Who cares about trivialities like sports after you've just seen a person so profoundly crushed, maybe for life? When you've lived this much complex trauma at this level there's a time for reflection, which can make you a better medic and a better person. A patient is a person, and they deserve our undivided attention, complete care, and respect.

12 October 1989. Springfield Suburb. We are dispatched with no lights and siren to the apartment for the 28-year-old female assaulted by her boyfriend who may still be on-scene. No cops available so we enter the apartment carefully; we knock first, but the door is open. I scan the room, my foot-long metal mag-light up on my shoulder, ready for clobbering should the assailant wish to strike again. I had seen too many of these scenes weekly. I knew the guy wouldn't be far.

The young woman is alone at the kitchen sink washing dishes as if everything is normal. I slowly approach and ask quietly if it's okay if we come in and talk. She nods, and I ask if anyone else is in the apartment. She shakes her head side to side—no.

"Can we sit in the living room?" I ask with my partner back at the door keeping an eye out. His preferred method would have been to abruptly instruct we should go to the hospital and be done. I can see this from the look he gives me, his eyebrow raised impatiently.

"No, I have to do these," she says.

"Work is good," I say from six feet away, deliberately giving her space.

"How can I help?" I say. There's no reply, so I give her some time. I can observe that she's tense, tremoring and having difficulty handling the plate she's washing. I can also see, despite her hair hanging down around her face, that her face is swelling and bruised. She's clothed in a sweatshirt, track pants, and slippers. Scanning the room, there is no signs of fight damage, but that's not always evident. I see no liquor bottles, drug paraphernalia, bottles, weapons, etc.

She coughs and grasps her abdomen like she's going to vomit but dry heaves, and I wonder about abdominal trauma. She begins to cry, and we sit nearby at the small kitchen table where I can see now that her whole face is swollen. I can see she's breathing fine, and her front teeth appear intact. I reach into my small orange bag, pull out an ice pack, and hand it to her without asking, which seems to make it more expected and acceptable.

"Did you get hit in the abdomen?" I ask—sticking to simple direct assessment questions in a systematic order to keep our discussion open and her mind at ease. No prying. I don't ask questions of who or why; no *who did this, what happened, was there a fight, why did he...?* My questions bounce around but in time I cover a full head-to-toe assessment without touching anything.

"He kept punching me in the face, stomach, back of my head... I couldn't get away."

"Did you lose consciousness?"

"No, I was getting dizzy, but, no," she says as I look at the back of her head with the flashlight, seeing no blood but a growing lump. I also see her ear is bruised, bright red, and her neck has an abrasion. She denies spine or neck pain. This only takes a few minutes so no delay.

"Okay, when you're ready, doesn't have to be right now, how bout we take a ride down and get that lump looked at?" I ask, which gives her time, allows her the decision, and to feel in control.

"He's not the first to do this... why?" she asks.

"This is all on him, not you. It's not your fault. I'm sorry you went through this. You shouldn't have to. We're here for you, and I will not allow anything more to happen. We're here."

My partner comes in. "I spoke with the police and they will meet us at the hospital. Do you have your keys to lock up?" he asks, and she points to where they are on the counter. We pack a few items she wants and go to the hospital where the nurses will be waiting. The hospital also has a team of staff who will assess for psychiatric trauma or sexual assault.

On the way to the hospital, she opens up a bit more.

"I prayed and prayed he would just stop and someone would come but no one did," she said sounding very much alone and disappointed.

"I know, our prayers aren't always answered on time. We're here, and there's really incredible nurses at the ER tonight; I mean these folks are friends, they're dependable, honest. They will take care of you. That's who you need right now," I said with confidence, and this seemed to instill some relief.

Attending these trauma patients takes tact, empathy, interpersonal skill, and training, but good values and spiritual characteristics help, too. A properly trained care provider can guide every movement and word, but if those come across as programmed or rehearsed, it absolutely fails at times. More stress is added. Good moral characters with spirit (of any faith) have all the innate values, and the natural, sincere, empathetic state of mind helps others cope with non-physical pain.

Psychological abuse is another manipulative evil I saw the signs and symptoms of too often. The regular and deliberate use of cruel words, non-physical actions, and torment to traumatize a person mentally, in order to confuse and control that person's every function is the epitome of evil. If I ever thought about condemning a perpetrator, it was on these scenes. Make no mistake, it was not always men and "testosterone" but women, mothers, grandmothers, parents, transgender; all people. I had one female victim who was trying to contact help, and I saw that her girlfriend had dismantled the phone and nailed the doors and windows shut so she couldn't get that help. I saw a daughter so traumatized by her mother's threats on her own grandchild that she had a stuttered speech.

I once had a foreign woman begging for help in silent code signs; she gestured with her hands behind her boyfriend's back. She made clenched fist gestures to her head. At the hospital we noted multiple cigarette burns on her body at different stages of healing.

12 December 1987. Springfield. On a cold winter night, I meet a young Asian woman outside her apartment with her brother waiting for our ambulance. She complains of sudden onset of "generalized" abdominal pain, nods her head yes to nausea. We had seen many people at that time for a stomach flu bug. She is about seventeen years old with the frightened eyes of a deer in the headlights; she will not remove her coat nor several layers of clothes to allow me to assess her abdomen. We transport her around the corner to the hospital with no cooperation from her. I leave her on a gurney in the ER hallway with a twenty second report and have to run out for another call. When we return, our nurse "Sheila" is laughing at me and pointing an accusatory finger. She demands a quick meeting in the nurses' station.

"Nice assessment of that young lady you brought us. Did you even talk with her much? Guess what her abdominal problem was?"

"I have no idea. She wouldn't talk with me, seemed scared," I say.

"Well, we just delivered her baby. She was almost crowning when she came in."

"What? She was pregnant—in labor?"

I feel stupid for not figuring this out on my own in the ambulance. Nurse Sheila patiently explains to me that it appears she hid the pregnancy from her parents but not her brother, who kept silent for fear she would be abandoned (along with the baby) by the family. Interviewing her brother, the nurses understood that in their Asian culture, it is often forbidden to have extramarital sexual relations, never mind a child. The nurses also understood that some women in this situation and culture attempt to self-induce an abortion (by traumatizing the fetus by punching themselves in the abdomen, being punched, and other harmful methods), although such signs were not found in this case. This young woman endured extreme mental anguish not knowing her rights here, about access to reproductive health resources, or how the family will respond.

21 December 1987. I am working as a basic EMT and bring in a five year old who had previously broken both legs. They were set in a A-frame cast (legs apart to form an A with crossbar). The child screams incessantly, and the mother appears to not care. I note this to the ER nurses in my assessment along with the fact that the patient—a child—is very dirty and the cast seems to be shredding apart. We consider reporting this to the state DPH as mandatory child-neglect reporters.

I still work as an orderly in the emergency room so I am working the next night when the same patient returns by ambulance with the mother.

I talk with the ER charge nurse about the prior transport just a day before. The nurse assesses the A-frame cast and finds live bugs in the cast scurrying out the bottom. The child's mother appears undisturbed when the nurse confronts her with the bugs there. The mother only sneers at us and refuses to answer questions. The charge nurse was fed-up with this blatant abuse and summoned the police, who sent detectives to investigate as soon as they could. I assist and attend to the child, trying to wash his face and arms while the mother refused to assist me. I ask somewhat frustrated, "What mother won't care for her own child?" to which she mocks me with look of surprise.

12 September 1999. I have a call in the x-ray department of an affiliated clinic across from the hospital. The call was to go upstairs to the x-ray department and see the technician "Sandy" about a child she is tending to there. The technician guides me to the back viewing booth to show me some films posted on the x-ray light illuminator boxes. The films clearly show both the child's leg bones are broken with multi-spiral breaks consistent with twisting forces. Sandy also explains that the patient was first brought to a private doctor's office in a suburban town and then the mother chose to bring him to this clinic and not the emergency room.

We make a plan for the technician to call security immediately to attend and escort the mother over in their car while I take the child from the car seat to go directly to the trauma room. I don't think I can move that fast but I have the child down the stairs and in the ambulance in seconds. We splint the child's legs in place, treat for shock, and transport immediately as I report to the physician on the radio.

At the emergency room, the doctors, care team, and police hypothesize the problem to be judged in a court. A relative may have been twisting the child's legs or swinging him around by the ankles to break the legs, and the mother may have been uninvolved. Whatever the cause, we are all appalled.

Why? Morality, Ethics, Philosophy, Science and Religion

I'm reclining in my ambulance and reading one of a couple books I picked-up at the used book store. My wife can attest I've been reading all the books on philosophy and religion I can get my hands on since we've been together. It's self-evident that I am trying to understand peoples' behavior and why I'm still working this job. I've been open to understanding all religions and even the agnostic philosophers theories. My questions are quite simple. What the hell is going on? That's what I want to know. Is immoral and unethical behavior on the rise or am I just a witness to too much in my position? I don't need to prove anything and have had nothing to preach. I'm an ambulance driver and medic. I am also a person licensed to heal the sick and if possible, prevent harm.

I read that agnostic and atheistic philosophers claim theists are always trying to justify human behavior so invented a super natural being or beings. I also note some justify our existence is not by design but based on the "mindless natural laws," acting on mindless matter? *I have some issues with this theory because the behavior I am witnessing is not mindless and anything but natural.* In fact, most of the arguments against the faiths are based on "evidence" or human social behavior. I find these arguments against the faiths weak. Another atheist (non-agnostic because he knows') claims that ethical behavior and morality are a human choice and therefore humans behave at their best naturally and must develop their own rules. Really? Is that not a contradiction? I do not see child abusers following any rules. From all these books it appears professors have been analyzing human social behavior for a couple hundred years and learned humans are how complex? As much as primates? I agree Phsycholgy is a great science but the "Analytic Attitude" appears stolen from scripture itself.

The science according to one agnostic: "Morality is not just something that people learn; it is something we are all born with. At birth, babies are endowed with compassion, with empathy…"* There is a growing number of published science journal studies and editorials that claim morality itself is scientifically "genetic" and therefore does not come from a higher or creative power or from religious learning and growth.

If we are born with the same innate morals that are an inherent element in ancient scripture of all the faiths and integral to spirituality, *then it makes sense that this spirit is created as part of the human soul.* Natural, inborn morals are not just taught and learned but explored and developed in all our major faiths. You cannot explore and develop or train such genes.

I think about these things because I'm trying to understand. If I cannot understand than I cannot help my patients as well.

Philosophers base their arguments against the existence of a supernatural power on a mix of theories including human social behavior, morality, psychology, and that proof is in sight or evidence. I can only conclude in a manmade world of violent evil blind men there is a God, because he is the only power at work against them. God's existence is in his creative work, the evidence is in it's evolution and will to thrive as I have witnessed.

EVOLUTION

As I begin working in the 1980's, medicine advances and becomes specialized and so do the transports. As an orderly, I don't know much, but I witness the demands placed on our staff as patients flow in from the smaller hospitals. We became the regional Level 1 Trauma Center and the only place to go for PCI, cardiac catheters and other specialized surgical and neurological services, not to mention the major birthing center, pediatric and neonatal units and a small burn unit.

As the options expand so do the demands to transport patients to other more complex facilities. Boston and Hartford hospitals offer many advanced services such as heart and organ transplants as well as advanced stroke treatments. For all our attempts at becoming a licensed, *critical care level transport* service, we never achieved that designation with our limited resources. Such a team requires the hospital based system to have multiple disciplines on-call, and with budget short-falls, that wasn't going to happen. This would become a repeated professional disappointment for me as I struggled to improve us as a regional group, regardless of service representation (the name on the ambulance).

We had to evolve and grow to keep with the demand.

7 June 1990. My first significant—and solo—critical care level inter-facility transport (IFT) is a middle aged guy at Springfield Hospital ER who needs a new heart. His wife and kids are present, and he looks seriously sick. The doctors had been treating him, but their efforts were coming to an end. One of the cardiologists pulls me aside after we arrive.

"Listen, this guy's heart isn't functioning anymore. He needs to go down to Hartford and have a heart transplant. We will show you all the treatments he has had in the last several hours, but this is really his last hope."

"Okay," I said. "What about taking a helicopter there?"

"Too late," he said. "They're not flying right now due to conditions so you guys can probably get him there in, what, 45 minutes or less?"

"Yeah, we can do that."

"Look, his family is all over him, and they want more time, but we've been defibrillating him several times with his rhythms degenerating as you can see. So, don't waste any time. Just package him up and get going. Understood?"

"Yes, got it."

We move swiftly, effortlessly, without appearing rushed. We introduce ourselves and explain that it's a busy day and we want to beat traffic to get him down there. That made sense because it was later in the day and the I-91 traffic south was notorious; however, he knew the real reason. We wheel his cot out of the code room, slide him over to our stretcher, connect our monitor leads, check his IV, hang a couple meds, and we're out the door without delay.

Our patient, Dave, is an affable guy—amazingly calm and brave considering his physician's clear prognosis and hopeless odds. Dave talks about how worried he is for his wife and kids and how would they cope while he endures through all of this and what if he doesn't make it? Who would take care of them? He begins to look distraught, distant, and troubled. I try to project a confident, positive, and defiant outlook in support of him, grasping his shoulder.

As our little ambulance that could chugs up the highway on ramp, Dave turns his head to me with one last plea for help, and then the reflected lights in his eyes dimmed.

"Dave, take a deep breath, cough for me, can you cough?" I instruct as I put the stretcher head down flat. I grab the cardiac monitor defib paddles (we didn't have disposable pads then) and look at his rhythm in a couple different leads. Pulse less V-Tac. I shock him a few times checking for signs in between—nothing. Now V-Fib. I began CPR by myself in the back.

"Hey, Dave's coded, can we get an assist?" I called up front to my partner, Joe.

"Fuck no, all the rigs are out, you know that," Joe said.

We were rapidly slowing down on the highway. "Look at this traffic," Joe called back. "Probably backed-up all the way down to the Connecticut line or even Bradley. At this rate it could take us an hour even with lights and sirens...no shoulder here and these assholes aren't moving. I could cut over to route five if you want, but it's probably just as jammed."

I continued compressions one handed, a couple ventilation assists with the bag valve mask and called our hospital on the C-Med radio phone, which reminded me of a kid's Fisher Price toy. "Yes, this is Unit 08, Medic 909. We are transporting the cardiac IFT to Hartford, and our patient has already coded. Patient went into V-Tac, unresponsive to defibs, now in fine V-Fib. Second round of ACLS meds given. ET insertion next. We are in heavy traffic looking at a possible forty minutes to an hour transport, unless we get police escort. Do you want us to continue? Please advise."

Joe pulls over to the side, jumps in back, and does CPR while I drop in the endotracheal breathing tube ETT, check insertion and lung sounds. Then our MC physician talks over the C-Med radio.

"MC 12 to Unit 08. Continue CPR and ACLS efforts and return to us. There is no point in transporting with his current loss of cardiac function. We will see you soon. Thank you gentlemen." His voice trailing off.

With that we continue to the next exit and back through the city to the emergency room. Some staff meets us outside, and we transfer Dave to the same room he left, and our MC calls the code. He announces the time of death.

"You guys tried; that's all you can do," he said.

Clearly, that was not the goal. But it is a strong example that shows if we had additional training, equipment, and IV pump medications running, maybe we could get the patient to the needed service. That became a personal goal of mine—because for the patient and the MC it mattered, but not the ambulance company. In fact, because the company could not bill for the added expense, they said it would only be a burden. This response only pushed my motivation to improve IFT levels of care forward. At each regional and departmental meeting, we noted our progress and mapped a plan to achieve next steps as we evolved as practitioners over the years.

21 February 2012. We arrived at the community ER for a 75-year-old female diagnosed by X-ray with a rupturing aortic aneurism. The RN states that the patient came in complaining of acute back pain for two days, followed by a chief compliant of "tearing" pain in her upper-mid abdomen today. Our patient was been given morphine and other extensive treatments by medics and the ER nurse with no relief, and it showed in her panicked expression. Her heart had to be PACED with an external pacemaker set at 80-90 beats per minute and this alone causes pain. Her movement was limited due to the pain. So pain control was another aspect of care to manage with opioid medication called hydromorphone running through an intravenous pump.

We transfer her to a stretcher and work to decrease her blood pressure to our target range by infusing the pressure lowering drug, two units of blood, and intravenous fluids, however resistant. I try a different approach with gradual success. Finally, we can decrease the blood pressure lowering medicine (Nicardipine) en route. We arrive, report to the doctor and nurse, and wheel her down to the OR together where surgeons and staff await gowned at their table.

What I didn't report to them or write in my report was the confidence I instilled by allowing her to pray in her faith, focus to get her B/P down. She suggested reciting prayers (to herself). Here was an example of clinical treatment (which is the cold, methodical science) applied with a strong amount of the patient's own faith, healing the patient. That is what I call a real EVOLUTION of care in the field.

I'm confident those prayers helped and had a role in stabilizing her for transport. But how do I know they helped? What if I just sat back and said, "Go ahead, pray away; what we really need to do is to get you there and you need to relax using this process." I've observed other medics and RN's say that. The result is the hopelessness and anxiety drive their physical condition downward. So can we instill confidence by command? No, confidence in medicine, people, and even yourself is limited. We've heard and tried all the tricks taught by self-help researchers and experts. They say "know yourself, face your fears, be grateful, meditate on relaxation, etc." That works on television and in controlled studies but not in near death. At the worst of times, you cannot fool anyone, including an atheist into having faith in those. We all know those fail every day. Meditating in prayer alleviates the burden and yes, there are researchers who claim it is the "science of prayer" process (physical act evoking a physiological response)—like yoga and meditation that provides the relief.

One published study from investigators declares "a physiologic state of deep rest induced by practices such as meditation, yoga, deep breathing and prayer" evokes the (desired) physiological changes such as blood pressure and heart rate" (Massachusetts General Hospital Institute for Technology Assessment 2013). Maybe that works in trials, and if it does help my patient, terrific. I have never seen that work on scene or in an ambulance. I've seen deep breathing make matters worse. I've seen people meditate on their breathing only to become anxious about their breathing. I have not seen healing yoga or mediation in emergencies.

Billions of people believe it is the higher power that created you that has the upper hand. To truly pray means to surrender your will to the will of a higher power, to God in Judaism, Jesus in Christianity, Allah in Islam (Islam means to surrender), Oneself and self-confidence in Buddhism, Guru (God in human form) in Hinduism, Great Spirit in some North American Indigenous Faiths. In context to surrender means simply to have faith beyond ourselves. Understanding what heals our patients can help them.

Inter-facility transports can be non-emergent stable runs. However, specialty care transports, critical care transports (CCT), intra-hospital transports, as they are variously known, are basically critical care runs with patients who are at times unstable or often go unstable due to the rapid changes. The range of illnesses, injuries, and ailments was limitless. Some of the toughest challenges included patients with unsecured airways who may need rapid airway interventions, patients going into forms of shock, acute respiratory distress syndrome with ventilation issues, uncontrolled bleeds, and any malady that required medications that we weren't accustomed to. Furthermore, the changes in equipment, and changes in environment affect patient condition and require adjustment and quick action. A knowledge of the pathophysiology (the disordered physiological processes that come from disease and injury) takes time and study to understand. We learned to better analyze, interpret, regulate, and problem solve to optimize the patient's condition. The bottom line here is called critical thinking. *This clinical aspect of care was one area we had to learn and grow.*

As I studied and learned from the physicians and nurses, it was the worst case scenario calls that taught us the greatest lessons. One critical skill was balancing a patient's stabilizing medications, such as the vasopressors used with sedation medications. While you treat a patient's hypotension and hemodynamics, the patient's system adjusts and reacts; thus, sedating the patient with even small incremental doses counteracts the effects of your vasopressors. Similarly, a patient lying on their back in misery on a ventilator does not wish to be fully conscious for the transport; so, assessing and optimizing the treatment is a critical clinical skill as much as any. The more of this work I did, the better I became at it—getting patients to their destinations alive and as comfortable as possible. This became a source of pride for me by 2000, even though I was not recognized with a commendation for medic of the year in my region until 2013. Usually, I never went to the regional functions and accepted such awards, but it was time.

When the medication Milrinone came on the scene, a new class of inotropic/ arterial vasodilator, it was cool to see improved medicine work for our patients with congestive heart failure. It improved contractility of the heart muscle and left ventricular diastolic relaxation to improve the heart's diastolic function. The drug improved outcomes for at least some of our heart failure patients, many of whom were on digoxin or diuretics. These patients often needed to be transported long distance to Boston hospitals, and it was these advances in medications that bought these patients' extra time.

These critical care level runs could be challenging given the intersecting and contradicting factors. One challenge was that I was often alone without another staff member or medic available to assist. There's a big difference between having resources at your fingertips (as at the hospital) to assist with decisions on everything: medication adjustments, rate changes to treat changing patient conditions, sedation, intubation, ventilator settings, pain management. Add in the elements of transport—weather, traffic, communication, changing patient condition, equipment malfunctions, distance—all these affect your work. The transport to Springfield was often twenty minutes, but an hour and a half to two hour transports to Boston was not uncommon. That can be a long time when you are alone in the back of an ambulance and your patient begins to deteriorate in front of you.

For advanced, "expanded-scope" IFT medics, it wasn't unheard of to be handed an unstable patient who was ready to "code on the road." This was no laughing matter for us because we all knew that the receiving facility, doctors, family and friends *all* expected the patient to arrive safely—and alive—despite all parties understanding the inherent risks. We knew they expected all to go well as it does on TV and the movies.

I did more than my share of critical care level IFT's and always met the challenge with a pre-trip plan. More often than not these patients could not be properly prepared due to staffing shortages, time, etc., and the job to improve the patient's condition fell to *me*, the transporting medic.

16 April 2005 Springfield. We arrive at the old city hospital turned rehab center for a 76-year-old man presenting with chest pain and shortness of breath (SOB). The nurse explains his past medical history (PMHx) including congestive heart failure (CHF) and diabetes (DM). She shows me his medications list. He is on insulin and some cardiac meds. I make quick notes for my report.

I walk into the old hospital room with the cracked walls and peeling paint. My patient is conscious, alert, and oriented (CAO), talking to me in whispers due to his weakness.

"I cannot breathe. My chest is killing me. Get me out of this place," he says.

He is in acute distress—weak and slumped over up on his hospital bed. The chest pain, he says, is ten out of ten—unbearable. He is unable to speak now that he's in such severe distress.

I need to rule out exacerbated congestive heart failure. I place him on the cardiac monitor to see bradycardia and the possible causes of his slow heart rate, which is causing the CHF. We must rule out cardiac muscle death, or myocardial infarction (MI). A quick 12-lead shows no heart damage or the progressing wave changes of injury.

I can see our patient is unstable, weak, pale, diaphoretic, and in need of immediate airway management and control of his slow heart rate. He has poor chest wall expansion—very shallow. I hear no wheezes with my scope. His lungs are auscultated with diffuse RALES in all fields. The right side of his neck has jugular venous distention / bulging (JVD) while he is sitting upright, which shows increased venous pressure. He is monitored in atrial-fibrillation at an irregular rate of 40 to 60. I can barely feel his radial pulses greater than 40. My partner, a basic EMT, is unable to hear his blood pressure with a standard b/p cuff.

We apply oxygen by a mask (NRB) at 100% producing O2 saturations to 94%. I pop in an IV in seconds. He doesn't move. We push meds including Valium and Versed to prepare and facilitate intubation. The patient needs a breathing tube. We assist ventilations with a bag valve mask by hand. I attempt intubation once, but the patient still has a clamped jaw. *Now nasal intubation is necessary to achieve an airway.* Without that breathing tube, he could become more hypoxic. I administer more sedating meds to relax him so I can pass the tube. I ease down the nasal tube on the second attempt. I bag valve ventilate in line with his cadenced breathing rate, which I talk him through, telling him when to take a breath. I have one hand on the bag valve mask and one on his shoulder as we do this together. He senses my assistance and I can see the relief.

I never let him feel alone as folks in these institutions are too often left alone, trapped in their own uncomfortable world. My words are chosen carefully to support him. I can see he is Christian from the tattered bible on the nightstand so I use words and terms he might recognize without sounding preachy. "All things are possible, so don't lose heart," and "Do not be afraid, be strong," His breathing becomes easier, and he gets some comfort from that.

Next, I apply pacer pads and pace externally with electrical capture at 120 amps, increasing his heart rate to 70.

I give him Nitroglycerine (NTG) spray and paste on his chest, Lasix IV to eliminate excess fluid in the lungs, Valium and Versed IV to sedate and intubate, and D50 for low blood sugar.

The patient stabilizes with the external pacing, medications, and breathing tube. To accomplish this, I had to earn his faith and trust in me and my skills, of which he knew nothing. I reflect if he could recall my supportive words, which had power if only from above.

In the early evolution of our advances for IFTs we had to advance our intubation and airway skills as well as ventilation skills using transport ventilators. Patient treatment problems could be exacerbated with the difficult airway. This is a sick person who has been entrusted in your care and the missed tube is not only uncomfortable, despite sedation but prolongs the struggle the patient experiences to breathe. Now the clock is ticking, and there is no back-up to assist in the second attempt.

As an example, a patient who has multiple problems (losing consciousness, airway unsecured, breathing difficult with heart failure, low heart rate due to bradycardia, and blood pressure dropping) needs cardiac attention and airway attention simultaneously. If we get sidetracked with the airway, then we are not providing the needed attention to the heart.

We had tried Rapid Sequence Intubation (RSI) with sedating and paralytic medications in the past, but it proved to be a complex system to maintain. Training is required constantly, and while it allows a quick airway, it is rarely needed. So, we stuck with standard sedation and even nasal intubations to keep it simple but still develop the advanced skills to handle the patients.

We trained constantly on the newer ventilators with advanced modes of ventilation. Training directly with the respiratory therapists at the hospital units was the best way to become proficient.

10:08. 12 May. 1990. We respond to a call for cardiac arrest. We arrive to find the patient laying supine in the grass with CPR in progress. Bystanders state the elderly patient was removed from his car pulseless and apneic. There is a scar on his chest from a heart bypass. His vitals are absent and his pupils are fixed and cadaveric. We ventilate and intubate him, which improves his skin coloration slightly. We administer epinephrine and atropine rounds every three to five minutes by IV. We defibrillate three times with Lidocaine and the patient goes back to a dissociated rhythm, sinus arrest, and flatline. This a typical pattern of responses to routine interventions. I had seen too many med pushes in this scenario with the typical result of death. Everyone has their day I guess.

We load in the patient on the cot and I hop in next to him. I look at him, bow my head, and make a quick but sincere sign of the cross as I often did when no one was looking. Most people might perceive this as a tacky display or an overt religious point. If anything, this simple, gracious religious gesture, which I was raised to perform, lifted my spirit knowing I was performing the most important thing I could offer the patient, which wasn't a plastic tube, medication, or shock.

The sign of the cross is a prayer in itself. As a sacramental, it prepares one to receive grace. Grace is a gift from the heavenly Father given through his son, Jesus Christ. This refers to the enabling power and spiritual healing offered through his mercy and love.

This also has more meaning than another injection of epinephrine.

Surprisingly, I see his pupils constrict slightly despite his pulseless rhythm and flat line on the heart monitor. Maybe it was a benign nerve impulse, but I had learned that the brain does not send impulses back to the eye in death. My partner moves nearer the monitor as I slide next to the patient's head taking over the ventilations. I pull his eyelids back and notice his dilated pupils constricting and trying to focus. His eyes focus for a fraction of a second on mine. I am speechless. Nothing has changed according to the monitor except as a result of our compressions. I ask for compressions to halt a second and feel for a pulse—nothing. I am afraid to check his pupils again but they are once again fixed and mid-dilated.

My partner asks, "Do you see something?"

"No."

But it makes me think. Why would his pupils attempt to constrict?

It was because of situations like this that I became more fascinated, with the idea of the presence of spirit absent of physical life. Pupillary response is a physiological response indicating life, and should not be present when a patient has died. I began to think of it as a sign that our efforts may have a supportive affect. That may sound far-fetched, but allow me to explain. This was not the first time I had seen the presence of life where it shouldn't be—maybe in response to the grace of a greater power. That was the only variable on scene from the typical code routine. This was incredible and perhaps unbelievable, which is why I usually mentioned nothing lest people think I was more delusional than they were. As for the pupil activity, I have replayed that image in my head many times since, and it defies explanation. The patient had been down and was clinically dead, even the ER doctors agreed. After the code was called at the ER, I asked a doctor about the possibility of that sign being the patient focusing on me and his thought was that it was a chemical creating a reaction in the optic nerve. Ask an experienced physician and they may have seen similar signs of pupillary reaction after death. Often these are chalked up to relaxation of iris muscles (which causes dilation) or even rigor mortis (mis-shaped). But thinking to myself, I couldn't deny what I saw—his pupils were focused on me, however briefly, and on a world he was leaving forever.

Let me share this thought. When you are born from apparently nothing to form into a complex human being that develops and thrives not just physically but spiritually on this spinning ball to experience decades of life among the living, how can you leave without one last look?

The first look of life into your eyes is certainly as important, and if you have ever attended a birth, especially for your own child, you know what I mean. When that baby opens their eyes and begins to focus on you, it is truly a magical moment, but why? Ask that question and you will probably get many different answers. Some say it's simply the innocence of new life, others say it's a miracle that life so fresh can enter the world with a lens open and ready to learn from sight. Considering the newborn knows absolutely nothing of this world and begins to explore it from those first seconds is absolutely amazing.

These concepts, along with the struggles of patients I cared for, changes me. I have grown clinically, but it is these experiences that forced me to take life more seriously, to evolve emotionally and spiritually.

I have thought of this more than most. We are titled "lifesavers" yet we are more often in attendance of death or near death. How can we ignore it, waiting to save the next one?

Once again, I see an opportunity to evolve our system and ourselves.

I think it is unreasonable, even ignorant, that not only scientifically but morally, leaders in health care and society in general have chosen not to explore this moment in greater depth. Why not? Why have we not placed investigators and researchers with high definition cameras to study this further? Instead, we use high tech cameras to study athletes playing with a ball. I suggest it is time we investigate a better approach to determine what supports are needed at the end of life. We could have a specialist on call to handle this aspect of EMS—a psychologist, a religious representative, or other expert. I am not suggesting there be any words required by the medic on scene. I doubt that most EMS folks have that motivation. I am suggesting we learn to determine what if any supports are desired and summon them if needed. Maybe this could be the beginning of conversations and studies between medics, patients, and their physicians around the globe.

A clinically trained medic would also ask *how that would help*? I'm not certain, but if you have ever been near that moment yourself or with someone you truly love; you might ask, "Couldn't the most meaningful words be more helpful to the patient than another IV bolus?" Of course.

How else could we evolve our care to improve the patient's experience?

Once, my coworker and I chose to play relaxing music at the patient's request on the way to the hospital. We had a tape box (yes, cassette tapes) of classical music, opera (who doesn't like Pavarotti?), and other assorted styles. We would ask patients what they preferred on the way in and play it for them. Most opted for nothing. Others would agree, somewhat reluctantly, but once their music was playing they were pleased and grateful. Other medics thought it was a distraction. We saw our "music therapy" as another level of patient care; it was certainly better than the sounds of sirens.

This practice could be extended to spiritual care. Maybe if spiritual support of that person's choice (all faiths have music, verses) were to be provided via headphones that could be helpful and calming. Another option could be to provide this as a treatment option as needed with the patient, who has it on their person ready for the emergency. This may not be a EMS option but a primary physician consideration with their patients. It would be another way for patient care to evolve with the help of modern technology and our growing understanding of how psychological or spiritual factors affect the physical.

CRITICAL THINKING
FOR CRITICAL CARE

When I began in the mid 1980's, the idea of civilian Medevac—military medical evacuation by helicopter or ground, born out of MASH units in the Korean and Vietnam wars—had lost its momentum here. ALS critical care level inter-facility calls were a rare event. At this time, we were very much alone and without leadership guiding the process. Everything I could do as a medic was a liability for me because the RNs and doctors often would not ride along. This was no fault of theirs because they had no support from hospital administration to do so. But the demand for this level of transport was increasing again. This became a complex problem that lasted most of my career and continues today.

As time marched forward we were trained to "monitor and optimize" more medications on the IV pumps, operate a transport ventilator with a respiratory therapist but not run blood or do much else that was invasive. We did run advanced classes we would later call "expanded scope" for paramedics. We brought in MDs to cover most of the core material: assessment, hemodynamic monitoring, respiratory, neurologic, shock, ACLS, trauma, pharmacology, gastro, toxicologic, obstetric, pediatric, intra-aortic balloon pump therapy, and sepsis. It wasn't a nationally recognized CCTP program. Even when I ran this as a hospital-based operations manager, we had no support from the greater medical community and a very small budget.

Looking back from the 1990's to today we never had the support that a great system requires, which is unfortunate. After all, we delivered the same patients that hospitals received funding for. I tried to garner interest but administrators believed the project a waste of their effort and money.

So, our small group of medics in western mass learned everything we could from the few Emergency MDs who could see our motivation was for *their patients.* That core group of physicians and nurses truly cared about their patients. Then, technology rocketed from the 1980's into the 2000's along with computers and cell phones. We gained improved portable cardiac monitors and ventilators. It inspired me to know we had the tools to help sick people. That is all I wanted to do.

28 January 2009. Hospital ICU to Boston Hospital ICU with a call for respiratory failure. A 64-year-old female presented with heart block. History of heart dysrhythmia atrial fibrillation, high blood pressure, and aortic tent (a spring type tube that keeps the vessel open for blood flow).

We arrive to find the patient in ICU but with added problems including an ulcerated trachea with deviation. The patient had been transferred from another hospital where they had placed a pacemaker to control her chaotic a-fibrillation rhythm. She had an endotracheal tube placed by rapid sequence intubation (RSI) and then extubated by the physicians. Airway managed with difficulty by the MD visualizing using a bronchoscopy scope to see grey/blue vocal cords, proving an ulcerated trachea. Carefully they reintubated with a smaller tube to get her to the next hospital safely. She was sedated with Propofol, and we are given a standing order to adjust that from 45mcg per hour to 55 mcg per hour.

I request to increase sedation as she is awakening with the road bumps; the increased sedation makes her comfortable. Awakening on a ventilator in the ambulance would be traumatizing. There is nothing you can say (such as a doctor joke) to make them happy or laugh in that situation.

The portable ventilator is set on assist control (AC) rate of sixteen breaths per minute, which can be adjusted for comfort. We keep our patient stable with the medicine adjustments as her b/p ran up and down unpredictably. She should have been an otherwise stable patient, but her discomfort from the reintubation prior to transport requires more medication, which in turn affects her stability. It is a *balancing* act on our part during transport.

Ideally, a critical care team consisted of a medic, MD, and RN or RT transport, but that rarely happened. Many transports we ran alone. Of course, per protocol we had the option to refuse transport without assistance, and the responsibility falls back on the hospitals, but then the patient doesn't get their advanced chance at survival—how caring is that? At times, medic and hospital staffing were both super tight, and a decision had to be made. The helicopters don't always fly in New England with our wonderful weather; so if it was raining, snowing, or sleeting, or even unpredictable with heavy clouds—forget it. Of course, these are not ideal conditions to drive on the interstate out to Boston either. Add to that the time of day, like rush hour traffic, and you have a long distance marathon. I certainly welcome a challenge, but I don't welcome the risk and liability. If something goes wrong between cities in the middle of nowhere, I was on my own. There are no "stat codes" called on the highway, no anesthesiologist to call up from the operating room. If the patient crashes, the receiving facility is going to ask why. I could be seen as at fault, even if the death was inevitable; we would be questioned and our license to work could be revoked.

Whenever a patient 'crashes' there are specific steps to take in specific scenarios, and each step needs to be completed, timed, and accounted for. For example, take a change in breathing when assisted by the ventilator. We assess the patient first, then the equipment. So, for the patient, we first might assess the level of consciousness/ sedation, airway, tube, and lungs. Then, we work from the mouth, tracing the vent tubing circuit back. It's protocol to disconnect the vent and bag ventilate the patient if the ventilation isn't tolerated. Then there are unseen steps that should have been taken to prevent patient deterioration as you departed the hospital or en route, minute by minute. There is a good amount of information the medic needs to know when transporting such critical care level patients for an hour to two hours. This increases with time such as for medics who work farther out in rural areas.

We knew core medication classifications and all the pharmaceutical aspects in detail. However, sometimes medications—like paralytics—were transported which we were less familiar with. A short term chemical paralytic is often used to place an airway and for patients who required ongoing chemical paralysis for transport. Its onset was quick at 60-90 seconds, but its duration of action was 45 minutes. Our transport time to Boston medical centers was an hour and twenty or longer in inclement weather. Either we had to re-medicate (re-paralyze) the patient or deal with the concerns with other classes of medications. This took careful consideration of our patient's condition and critical care with the sending and receiving physicians.

The goal with these transports is to get the patient to the Intensive care Unit or operating room alive and in best shape as possible. Keeping the patient calm and talking them through the pain to keep their blood pressure down is key. However, like all patients in acute pain with poor prognoses, you have to convince them everything is going to be okay. To do that, you yourself have to believe it. Of course, if you don't because you're a faithless slug who believes a scientifically hopeless situation is immutably hopeless, then the patient in this hypersensitive state is going to read you like a flashing neon sign at night Once again, having some faith helps. It also helps not to be too serious. Believe it or not—I do have a sense of humor, however dehydrated. I may say, "Now we're arriving at the hospital in about five minutes, no, maybe ten, no, could be twenty. When we get there and transfer you to your bed, the nurse is going to say to you, "the doctor will be with you in a minute." That usually gets them to smile if they can. A patient may feel fragile and need supportive words or may feel angry and wish to express their anger in their own words. *Words are treatment like the medicine and need to be balanced as well.*

I have seen other medics (along with nurses and doctors) work in a hopeless mental state, dragging their patients down with them, and it has clear effects: poor outcome or death. When assisting other medics, I've often witnessed them say the most hopeless things in the most obvious ways: verbally and with palpable emotional tones, facial expressions, body language, etc. Basically, these medics suck, and I have often been very verbal myself in telling them so. A number of times I have relieved them, taken over patient care, and even thrown a few out of the bus.

20 February 1993. We arrive at a mobile home trailer on the side of the road about 30 minutes away from our city hospital. An old pick-up truck outside tells me this may be a working class, no-nonsense person. The 78-year-old patient with graying hair and beard is seated in the living room complaining of tearing abdominal pain with signs and symptoms (S&S) consistent with an aortic aneurysm. The EMT turns to me and says," Nothing we're gonna do for this." I step in, reach over and palp the patient's abdomen and find a pulsating mass the size of a grapefruit. The EMT shakes his head side to side with a grim face; his performance is not only useless but makes the patient's situation worse. I look at the pale patient absorbing this whole hopeless assessment. He looks absolutely terrified because he thinks he is clearly a dead man, according to this jackass. How difficult would it be to simply communicate with him some hope in consideration of the patient's thoughts? Is it really that difficult to ask a few questions and provide some comfort?

I take over the assessment and treatment. First, I assure him that we will relieve him of some of his pain and get through this. With a firm hand on the patient's shoulder, we count through his breaths aloud. My partner, Hope, and I carry him out and into the ambulance, where she asks the medical history questions and sounds nicer doing it than I do. As give him pain meds in the rig and encourage him to focus on whatever makes him feel better. I ask if he has any faith he wants to talk about, and he tells me he wants to say some prayers to himself as that comforted him. I hold his shoulder reassuring in support. We make it to the hospital and they whisk him downstairs to the operating room.

After the run I followed up with the hospital docs to see how the patient did and if we made the right decisions. Usually the feedback is great; at other times, they may correct us on something we did or did not do. In this case, the doctor said we did well in finding the mass and made all the right treatment choices. The doctor also added that the patient commented he felt "he was in good hands."

DIFFERENT RELIGION,
SAME VALUES

17 November 1988. When Elana and I enter the spacious home, we don't know what the complaint is, just a call for assistance. It is yet another shift on a string of cold, rainy days and a seemingly never-ending cycle of bad luck. We recently had a high school football player broke his neck on the field, and our spirits have been low ever since. We are in a rut.

We shuffle into a large living room filled with an entire Indian family; the elderly mother is in the adjacent room. I feel out of place in our dark blue cop-style uniforms; the family is all dressed up, and the women are wearing beautiful, colorful clothes. The son informs us the mother is dying but will endure the suffering because it could change her "bad karma." They are followers of Hinduism, and their belief is that spiritual suffering is connected to karma. He knows she would not want to go to the hospital in these last hours. He only asks that we assess her respiratory condition.

The sight of an entire family—over a dozen members—surrounding their dying matriarch in loving support warms my heart. The son notes a few relatives had even come in from New York. I watch as they tend to her; she accepts only water to drink. Framed pictures of extended family adorn every surface. Friends and family brought pans of prepared foods, which line the kitchen. It reminds me a little of how Catholics come to the house of sick family members with homemade foods so the family can focus on caring for the ill. To say their religion matters at this time is an understatement.

When talking with the son and family, they make us feel welcome. After we finish our assessment, we talk a little of their religious beliefs. The son briefly explains the soul, *atman*, is eternal, and when the physical body dies, the soul is reborn in another body or attains release "moksha" from this existence. The continuous cycle of life, death, and rebirth is *samsara*. Rebirth is governed by *karma*. These ancient religious beliefs alone gain my attention and respect. Elana and I leave the scene and talk all evening about what we learned from another religion, and spiritual culture. It lifts us from our rut and sparks my curiosity to study more of other religions for life.

I am not a theologian, and this book is not written to preach any specific religion. This is about what worked for me and my patients. In many examples, spirituality seemed to be a factor. We all know from history and everyday events that bad things happen to good people regardless of their faith or how much they pray or how positive their attitude may be. Prayer certainly does not work that way. We can all think of mass atrocities that account for much suffering and death, regardless of the victims' innocence, faith, or prayers. I don't think my spiritual good will and works are solely miraculous. I do know one thing for certain. After treating thousands of people, I have made a difference and that many of my patients would have suffered more or be dead without me. A good works theology may do nothing for saving my soul, but it certainly has saved lives.

Having faith in God gave me a purpose and a mission; without which I would never have stayed the course. If I have been deluded, only to find the outcome of that delusional plight has still been the work of God. To say it is all random makes no logical sense. To say it was science and technology or the "Big Bang" is laughable to me. You can't get something from nothing. If I set off a ton of dynamite, what do I get? A giant void, nothing but broken elements.

My efforts were always a tireless continuum, minute by minute, year by year, and deeply anchored in faith in God. It was more than a positive attitude channeled into physical effort to gain a positive outcome; it was *listening for what needed to be done*. I knew what needed to be done without scripture, stories, and my religion—although I cherish all of that—just as some indigenous peoples gained knowledge by listening to the Great Spirit over the history of time. We don't need to memorize every single name, place, or date in scripture to know right from wrong. Too many people question every detail of history—each detail of each religious difference—but dare not accept the common values, seeking answers to unanswerable questions. We need to write our own stories from truths we are experiencing today.

I did not learn all I know in EMS from a college program but from the demands of daily work life dedicated with purpose. Other cultures learn in this manner, too.

1 March 2005 Springfield. A young man of Native American decent traveled here to see a friend from a reservation area out in the north western United States. He had found some trouble and may have broken his leg. He called us from the bus station at which he waited with the locals. In the ambulance we assess the leg with no major issues found, just spilt the lower tibia in a Fracture Pack splint with some ice. We had some time to talk on the ambulance ride and he spoke briefly of his home and reservation. He didn't care to discuss family. I asked if his tribe was religious or spiritual and he said there was a large number of Christians and missionaries; but his tribe did not want to mix faiths and believed in their native Great Spirit; (which was more a spiritual force than a being.) He described "problems" between the tribe (authorities) and non-Native missionaries; which made sense to me. He described their communal life values were the same as a Christians but they didn't need to be told how to live. He noted his reservation was 'run down' because he said no one owns the land and there's no place to work. We had similar interests in Spirituality and the Sacred. We agreed that anything ceremonial or historical gets lost when a different people try to impart their religious traditions on the indigenous. I could empathize with the situation and his frustration. However down; he was determined. When I left him at the orthopedic room, I wished him well and to be true to his own beliefs.

14 October 2007 Suburb of Springfield. After an IFT, I met a member of the North American native Anishinaabe Tribe (Ojibway). She was a strong woman in her fifties. Discussing her culture she explained the

Seven Grandmother/ Grandfather teachings are said to be: wisdom, love, respect, bravery, honesty, humility, and truth. I discovered that the spiritual foundations of this native culture are learned primarily by experience rather than placing the emphasis on academic data and information. For teachers the tribe relied on children, elders, spiritual entities, plants, and animals. We can all benefit in different ways of learning from such a culture with similar values.

9 May 1989 Springfield. We arrive at a first floor apartment for a woman who was in full term labor. We walk into the large house apartment to find about a dozen family members gathered around a young mother who has just delivered her baby maybe ten minutes prior. The mother is sitting on the blanket strewn floor covered and cradling her infant to her breast. She is in no apparent physical distress. The family of all ages are seated or lying about on furniture as if this is a fun family event. I assess the mother and newborn who both appear to be healthy. The mother speaks English and confirms the umbilical cord has not been cut nor the placenta delivered. The family is from Vietnam and confirms for me that home child birth is the normal delivery practice back home in Vietnam. These "natural births" or "Lotus Births" were common as the family points to a couple younger siblings who were also delivered at home.

As we make her comfortable on our stretcher I explain my concern with the safety of the practice as I know these home births can be injurious or fatal when complications occur. The mother just smiles and says she understands but that she had exams, was prepared by her physician and used a sterile technique. I do not dare lecture as it is not my position and accordingly make those notations for the hospital we are going to.

On the transport I allow her to share her happiness with me of the successful birth of her new baby boy. She is apparently a Buddhist or some form of that religion. I can only ask so much in this moment. We shared some values on the joy of her "happy baby" as she calls him. She says she has been eating well so that she can take good care of him. In choosing to deliver at home, I learn she is accepting of whatever the natural outcome is. While I am very hesitant to accept this approach, I am a paramedic, I must respect her courage; which comes from her religious and cultural perspective. She is a mother with two beautiful children at home. As I listen to her and watch her glow with her newborn I struggle with the possibility that I could have walked into a breech birth or birth with bleeding complications as I have seen by even that time. Still, she sits before me calm and confident with her happy baby. I know nothing of this religion or culture but I wonder if she has attained what they call 'equanimity' as she appears to be so composed in this situation.

STEADFAST

They call me T Val. I earned this abbreviated title so that I could be summoned as quickly as needed. Medics had nicknames here in the early years because we had a few Toms and Jims. I prefer Tom over an acronym but I'm proud to know that I was wanted to get certain things done. If there was an incident in town that called for experience that was how they would call me over. But I didn't possess any lightening skills others don't have. We're all certified, like beef. So what did I do to acquire such demand for dispatch? When you are in demand because of talents you have they're not all learned skills or all natural. It's a combination of many things. To do this job well was a decision I had to act on. To develop from within I had to learn how to improve my performance in every way. To do that I had to work in the busiest area on the busiest truck I could find. I tried Hartford and Boston as well but there were too many medics and not enough demand. I had to stay where I was needed most. Sure, many left in the early years but some stayed and some worked nearby for different FD departments. I liked the autonomy of a smaller system that was in fact, broken…that's correct. If everyone knows it's broken you can fix it, and we fixed it daily making it efficient. Unlike a larger system where everyone thinks it's great, and none are great; you are not allowed to improve it. I saw every second of every day as an opportunity to learn and grow. That concept came from religion, where God maintains all by the second. I learned to be an active listener before reflective listening became popular. I learned the four types of listening: appreciative, empathetic, comprehensive and critical before they became an academic focus. This path changed my youthful and wayward attitude. Others not on my path also changed my attitude.

It is tiring enough to develop your own attitude to evolve your skills and patient care without worrying about another practitioner's impact on your patient, or family. Education and skills are the least of our problems. We need every care provider to apply the same good attitude and values to accomplish a clear mission. If one's attitude of mind is unwavering on patient care, then their area of *aptitude* should be obvious. Your aptitude is your natural abilities and cannot be taught or bought through education. It should be found early in life so that you can gravitate toward your strengths. The idea that knowledge will save the world is debatable. There is an overabundance of information available today, such that no one person can recall all and apply it affectively. Many do carry it all around in their laptop or tablet and believe that the more knowledge they possess (in their hand if not in their head) the smarter they are. This approach to healthcare seems to be their entire existence. I found when it comes to clinical care, it is often the *ethical attitude* that inspires one to assess the situation effectively and come to sound decisions.

While it is my desire to share the relevant, good stories of patient care done on a magical level, I cannot ignore the nightmares I have witnessed. The following cases completed my training on how NOT to treat people. They put into perspective the damage a simple bad attitude can have from even the most skilled and educated of our nation's colleges and universities.

From a young age, I watched intently as the inept and the wicked surely tried to kill my entire family at a variety of local hospitals. My brother was hospitalized from a young age several times a year. My second home was the hospital, usually in a worn corner chair of his room. While some of the staff were saints and gave their all to make my brother comfortable, there were those who enjoyed watching him suffer while mounted on their high and mighty attitude to judge what exactly they would do. Regardless of what they knew should be done in critical moments that could result in greater suffering or even death; they would often choose to do nothing. Sounds unbelievable I know, but it's true.

1979 Massachusetts Hospital. I sat holding my brother in his room on the pediatric floor. The general atmosphere was full swing disorder. I was about 15 years old and had come in to see Doug, all skin and bones at about 45 pounds and dropping. He had been given liquid nutrition for days but was dehydrated and needed more fluid. I heard the nurses whispering at their station across the hallway. Evidently they didn't anticipate the poor acoustics of their voices bouncing off the vintage green wall tiles. I could hear how they were disgusted that the family of this kid was keeping him alive in his desperate condition.

"What's the point? I wouldn't want to live like that," one nurse said.

"I know. Just look at him," said the other.

So, that summed up the hospital staff's moral and ethical view in two sentences.

I guess they hadn't known my brother on a good day when he would communicate with us on his communication board or laugh and play in his wheelchair in our backyard by the stream. I sat listening in disbelief that they couldn't have some faith (that's FAITH as in complete trust or confidence in something). Did they think I wanted to see him here in this tiled prison, crying and moaning in such physical and emotional distress? Did they not understand that pain is a transient part of life, and we all strive to get through it for reasons beyond material happiness? Did they grasp that we needed their help?

A doctor walked up, leaned into the nurses' station, and started flirting with them. As he left, he said, "Now with Douglas, let's keep these fluids running." With that he knocked on the counter and made some hushed comments. They all laughed as he left.

A few minutes later, the nurse walked in with the typical pulled face on. She reached over and shut the IV pump off.

"He's had enough for now," she declared, turning sharply to walk out.

Now I was only about fifteen years old, but I knew what dehydrated was. Doug's mouth was as dry as sand, and I heard what the doctor had ordered.

"He's thirsty...can he get some..." I asked.

"No," she cut me off.

I reached for the water cup and began dripping small drops into his mouth. He smacked his bone dry lips on the drops and choked a little because he was too dry to swallow and the water hit his windpipe. The nurse came to the door with her hands on her hips staring in at us with the frustrated look of a higher authority whose orders were ignored. At that moment I was ready to snap. I had spent enough years attending my brother here and watching these empty corpse staffers who couldn't apply an ounce of kindness to their work.

"WHAT ARE YOU LOOKING AT?" I bellowed.

She walked away, too wrong to object, too stupid to counter, too weak to fight. Incidents like these fanned the flames of my anger. It was here that I learned to hate; and hate is a good thing when it is used to help the sick. Over the years there would be many such circumstances where manipulative and wicked attitudes would affect my brother and even my entire family. I learned to be a steadfast advocate firmly fastened to the bedside when needed.

October 2003 Massachusetts Hospital. I was working on the ambulance when I received a call to transport a male patient off the first floor medical unit back to my brother's group facility. Well, that had to be my brother because he was the only resident at the hospital I knew of. But it didn't make sense because I had just visited a day before and knew he was sick with pneumonia. My partner and I arrived well before pick-up time in uniform and decided to take in our stretcher in case it was another patient.

We wheeled our stretcher up to the nurses' station. I gave a polite smile and said we were there to pick-up a patient going to the group home.

The nurse responded in an extremely frustrated tone. "Oh, that one in 132. You can have him. This family is such a pain in our ass you would not believe it. His mother is in there trying to give *us* orders. I can't stand this—"

"Stop," I said in a low, controlled, and patient tone.

"No, seriously, these fucking people have no idea. She's so demanding."

"Stop. Stop. Please. You're talking about Mrs. Valentini?" I confirmed.

"Yes," she replied.

"She is my mother…that you're talking about."

"Oh." The nurse was speechless and confused, mouth hanging open. I could see the wheels turning.

"Yes, I'm Doug's brother. And I don't appreciate your opinion of my family. So, call the doctor in now to meet me at the room and see what this is all about."

"I'm so sorry. Yes, I'll get her now."

I went down the hall to the last room, and there was my mom in tears with her son pale and lying in shock in bed. My instincts kicked in as I assessed him. I could see he had no oxygen on or IV fluid running, but his vitals were all terrible—tachycardic, hypotensive, retractive, gurgling respirations, and O2 saturations in the low 80's. What the hell?

My mother began explaining that the staff said they couldn't do anything, but she knew he needed oxygen and IV fluid. She pointed to him lying there, "He looks so helpless. Can't we use those?" she asked pointing to the bags of IV fluid.

I placed an O2 mask on his face from off the wall O2 regulator, opened it up, and began to look at the IVs. The doctor walked in looking like the Wicked Witch of the West with a tangled mess of long gray hair and a face only another witch could love.

"Hello. What are we doing here?" she said in a low tone, annoyed at having to deal with commoners like us.

"Hi, I'm the medic who has come for the transport. I'm also the brother who wants to know why he's lying here in neglect and struggling with no support?"

She looked down at the floor and then up as if pondering this calamity at a lofty level and trying to find words we could understand. "Look, I reviewed his chart, and he has a long history of battling these respiratory infections. There's only so much we can do."

"So that's it, that's your assessment and treatment here? He looks in shock, and he can't breathe. I think we can help him with his breathing, and he's clearly in need of some fluid." I started moving the IV tubing and assessing his IV site.

"Don't—"

"If you don't treat him, I will. I'll push him in this bed right down to the ER and have a doctor treat him there."

"Okay, we will try some more IV fluid, but he's had a lot and his lung fields are congested."

"Good, do it now," I said matter-of-factly as the nurse came into the room.

With the oxygen and a couple liters of IV fluid, he bounced back and looked better within the hour. They hung some antibiotics and reassured my mother. They feigned concern but said nothing to me.

Sometime after, I wrote a detailed letter to the president of the hospital explaining the lack of concern and intentional disregard for life saving measures, in lieu of personal opinion on if my brother was worthy of those simple efforts. He never responded.

03:00am October 1985. I was a young night orderly and my grandfather had been checked into the same hospital. I went upstairs at some unforgiving time between one and three a.m. to check on him. Maybe he was awake having trouble sleeping, I thought. I walked by the glassed-in nurses' station unnoticed, where four nurses sat gabbing away, eating snacks, laughing. I pictured my grandfather up with a *Life* magazine, reminiscing about the old days with a nurse keeping him company. To my surprise and disgust, I found him in a dark room tied down supine in four point restraints, sweating profusely, and gasping for air with quick snoring respirations.

I put the lights on above the bed headboard and tried talking with him, but he was unresponsive, just trying to breathe. I hurried back to the nurses' station.

"Hey, why's my grandfather tied down and alone in his room? He's having some trouble breathing," I said.

"Why are you here after visiting hours and who allowed you in his room?" the nurse responded sharply.

"I work here too, will visit as he needs me, and you will take care of him now, or I'll get security up here,"

"Calm down," she said. "He's fine. It's not as bad as it looks. He has to be in restraints for his own safety and is just having some difficulty sleeping. I'll take care of it." She stomped down the hall to his room.

She assessed him and took off one wrist restraint, noting he looked a "little rougher" than when she last checked him.

"Was that when you tied him down to go eat and play games?"

She shook her head as if I were unable to understand the complexity of the situation. I removed the restraints. She placed a nasal cannula with low flow O2 on his face. I noted that his respirations weren't right; she agreed, began the protocol, and called the doctor, but each step was met with resistance and denial that anything was wrong.

He never returned to his normal baseline mentation and died soon after in the ICU. I like to think he was more comfortable there when he passed away, but I just don't know.

Is this really "advanced" care? Please, tell me what level of care this is? These incidents are hard to fathom but they are all real, and once again we must learn our lessons and not repeat them.

12 December 2009. I stand before the 78-year-old man in the hospital bed at his home on hospice care. He is suffering his last day with pancreatic cancer after weeks of battling against it, and I was called to the scene. He refused the morphine offered because he wanted "to keep my memories of my life and family, to go with me." He is writhing in intense pain, and the agony is visible in his eyes. His lungs, filled with fluid, are audible with course rhonchi indicating it will not be long. His wife stays by his side. I can see the support from family but not from hospice or his church priest at this hour. The man dies with his own spiritual confidence and grace intact to the bitter end, despite his bloodshot eyes that cannot hide the pain and disappointment with this end-of-life moment. Despite all my experience in comforting the suffering, I am useless in those last hours to this man who was my father.

My Dad was my friend as well as my father. You would not know he was a man of faith in talking with him because he was a very private person. I don't wish to think of his last days because he did so much for so many during his life. Family— his wife and two sons—meant everything to him. His tireless and loving care for his son Douglas was an enduring inspiration for me. His faith was present in his heart for him when nothing or no one else could help.

Working together for the relief of pain and suffering, in closeness with God is possible. But can we decrease healthcare costs while improving statistics?

There are healthcare professionals who would disagree with me on our responsibility to alleviate all forms of suffering. To some this is a business, an industry where we need to cut costs and improve the bottom line. I'm a manager so I do understand maintaining a budget in our survival of the fittest world. But there is a line, and we crossed it years ago. That has produced an attitude that wavers from the original focus of health care.

When patients are suffering, even dying, the general opinion is that we are not gods, there is nothing more to be done than the scientific solutions we have now. Oh well. That is an opinion I've heard from many outside the conference room, and it's not that they are all coarse people who don't care; I think it's a combination of their "realist" scientific view, their knowledge of the limitations on our resources, and maybe a lack of faith. I have held the same opinion myself at times. However, for our patients and the greater good in our communities, I like to provide the most relief we can for as many as we can. Not all providers have seen as much suffering as I. If they did I think they would agree it must end. If we do not commit to this, then are we not contributing to it?

There are many articles written about how we can implement a higher level of care based solely on advanced medical education. Some self-professed experts tout how utilizing a hybrid Physician Assistant (PA) or RN trained as a paramedic could resolve many issues. A new "super medic" if you will. I do not completely disagree. But I've seen such trained individuals attempt this transitional hybrid approach only to disappear from the project in short order. One night they find themselves at a shooting, covered in brain matter while being threatened by the corner bully. Surprise, Jack and Jill are back up the hill to work inside the cozy hospital suite. Being a paramedic is not exactly the idea of a dream job. People naturally gravitate towards an occupation that is challenging, rewarding, and safe. They don't want the excessive, ongoing risk to life and limb. I don't blame them. So why do we repeat this process?

And what's more, how many advanced techniques can you bring into the field before you just bring the patient to the hospital? Does this type of education address the problems of complete care I have outlined in this book? In my experience, it's just more science and toys, and neither will make a difference.

On the other hand, we could use more *diversely trained* people with the skills and education I'm taking about. So, I'm open minded about having more resources—from physicians, PA's, RN's, to psychiatric professionals, palliative care providers, and yes, even religious practitioners. Why not, they were in the field first for hundreds of years.

I once worked with a Friar who was an EMT in the field. He belonged to a religious order in the Catholic Church. Most other EMTs thought his lifestyle was weird and kept their distance. They never attempted to know him and understand his attitude. He had devoted himself to certain causes with his mind steadfast on doing good work. I'm not advocating we all become Friars, of course, but understanding their attitude is a good way to set your own expectations.

TIME, ATTITUDE, AND HEALING

Since I was a child I always loved pocket watches and grandfather clocks. There's something innately special about measuring time by the second and being aware of it moment to moment. I learned from my childhood experiences with my brother and then from EMS that "seconds are long." This can be good or bad, depending on your situation and sometimes your attitude.

For example, when you take that little coffee break outside at a small table to escape from work. Many of us think it is the coffee we love and savor (or the cigarette, wine, beer, etc.) But if you think about it, the coffee is merely a substance like all the others I noted that can leave you with a headache, sour stomach, or a cough in the case of the cigarette. So, is it the coffee you are enjoying or the time?

The break in itself is like a ritual. A ritual is a sequence of activities using words, actions, gestures, or objects performed in an isolated place. The ritual of stopping your work to sit still, sense or focus on something good, feeling good, may just be enjoying those seconds that are otherwise fleeting when you work. To do that you enter a state of mind and seize the moment, which is done by changing your attitude. If your attitude were negative or angry, the moment would be broken. In effect, this is the same attitude one has to correct when in meditation or prayer. It is a skill anyone can learn and apply.

You do not need to become religious, change your religion or strike a prayer posture reciting mantras (although that could be good.) Once again, this is just to enter a good state of mind. That might be empathetic, healing or even medicinally corrective.

I have found that when I apply this same attitude and approach to caring for my patients at the appropriate time, it has a healing effect. If a healthcare provider could apply this attitude with their patients regardless of whether they are religious or share the same belief or faith, then they too can learn new ways to heal. Give yourself a break from the mundane and try this in a steadfast approach.

PERSEVERANCE

As I write this we are well into the COVID-19 pandemic. It has been a tiring road, although our area was not hit with the patient numbers of New York or New Jersey. The stress of dealing with this threat has been compounded as I worry about my healthcare providers as a manager. We review our safety procedures and equipment around the clock, and I am exceedingly proud of the courage my people have shown. I'm not inclined to give us the hero title, as I reserve that for others, but courage in the face of death is noble regardless of the intensity, means, or field. The dangers of transporting COVID positive patients are very real. Some patients are on ventilators, in the confined space of an ambulance box, and some are transported long distance for hours. Some medics have fallen sick, but fortunately none in my group have been critical. What will it take to persevere with these new tests of our adaptability?

For the EMS worker, COVID 19 poses not only additional risk but the challenge of caring for people in full PPE (Personal Protective Equipment). First there is our practical skills performance but applying patient emotional support as I have been suggesting over the years is now more difficult—but not impossible. We have often had to wear PPE over the years for toxic emergencies, poisonings, unknown caustic substances, and communicable diseases, but this is different. Both our patients and us are now meeting, interacting, and basically living under layers of obstructive gear. It is much more difficult to make eye to eye contact, read the patients facial expressions, exchange a smile or words of support, and listen and hear your patient.

Everything I have noted regarding support to our patients over the years requires direct, one on one, personal communication and interaction—preferably unobstructed and with little interference. We have always faced challenges in difficult environments as in environmental emergencies, vehicle wrecks, industrial sites, and highways. But even in those situations, at times you can shroud your patient or support them once you get into the patient compartment of the ambulance. You could get close to communicate, but lately we've been unable to offer this small comfort.

With COVID-19 demanding so much PPE, the obstruction of personal interaction is never ending through the call. Therefore, we must be creative and do more to improve that. I read that one nurse created a mask with a see-through window over the mouth so a deaf patient could read her lips. With such masks all patients could read our lips and interpret our facial expressions. It is this type of improvisational thinking that we can all improve and personalize care.

A doctor in Italy said the hardest thing about caring for his COVID patients in this pandemic was seeing them die so alone in the isolation rooms. He watched so many moved for the final treatments to the quarantine unit away from family and friends. These patients often knew that they would not see their loved ones ever again as they were getting sicker and knew they would be all alone in the end. Apparently, he and some staff began using cell phone and computer tablets to allow family and friends to communicate with the patients in the isolated units and during their last hours. I think their improvisation to connect their patients to the ones they loved in this manner was nothing short of heroic given their overload of critical and dying patients even with limited staff.

These are examples of persistence in patient care despite great difficulty and that is perseverance.

My experience is that it does not take a college degree to provide the skills needed for the field—although college is the best place for a paramedic program. As for advanced training, I think hospitals are the ideal location when possible, as they have the patients and personnel to learn from. I learned more in the ER staff break room than I ever learned in a classroom.

I always kept my questions from the tougher cases in a small notepad. Over a coffee, I could ask the staff questions from the last case if they were open to it. Technical scenarios on longer trips with medications are good to cover and review. But whatever was inspirational for recovery was the better subject.

As an ambulance company manager, I was tasked with finding and training good medics. First, I had to find the right character. It all depends on the *person*: who that person is, what inspires them, and why they want to do this. I always sought a medic with the right attitude, integrity, values, mental and physical skill sets developed over a lifetime of relevant experiences. Folks like that are rare. All this comes from within; they must have the ability to persevere against all odds. If the person is of faith, I think that not only instills moral values but also inspires a person to persevere to accomplish their goals in that mission.

I'm not a fan of short, fly-by-night paramedic programs. These one to two year programs are popping up across the country—even online—and appear to produce ill trained medics with too little in-person experience. Think of that, a program designed to produce a bunch of technicians who will probably fail as many as they save—in spirit, mind, and body.

It takes more than students expect to make a good paramedic and a system that can provide decent care to all those we serve. Recently that has been neglected in our society as students opt for newer, more promising careers. Many students today *don't want the experiences* it takes to be a good provider; like starting off as an orderly.

My journey and training began as a big brother who had to learn all the responsibilities of caring for a medical patient who was much more than that—he was my flesh and blood, my very essence of being. Day in, day out, year after year, I learned not only the technical and physical aspects but the emotional skills to apply and develop true compassion and integrity. Those skills work in combination with critical thinking, problem solving, collaboration, and communication (yes, sounds like a class.) Ultimately, all of these skills are used in research, management, and leadership. Simultaneously, I learned from my parents about teamwork, commitment with dedication, and the power of love and spirit.

As I grew up, I learned about hard work with my hands and my head from my cousins and uncles on both sides of my family. From business to construction to repairing cars, I learned to focus and get a job done, regardless of obstacles, using practical skills and ingenuity.

I learned from living on my own at a young age and being self-reliant to never wait for anyone when the going gets tough. I learned driving a tow truck as my first real job, which may sound trivial, but if you can winch a crashed truck up a thirty foot embankment at night in a snowstorm, flip it over, and then tow it and back it up into a crowded city impound yard, then you can drive an ambulance across a city without accidents for years to come. Driving is one skill they don't teach you in college. I worked as an auto mechanics assistant, which years later allowed me to keep a fleet of ambulances running. Each job was a classroom in itself, and the people I learned from were the most inspiring teachers.

Attending my paramedic program in college, I learned from every person involved as I grew personally and professionally. I worked in hospitals as an orderly and eventually a manager. There wasn't a technician, nurse, or doctor from whom I didn't learn at least one lesson. I worked in a hospital neurology lab conducting EEGs and polysomnographic studies, always learning how the brain works from a clinical perspective. Who knows better about that than a neurologist? I worked in a few EMS systems and managed a couple over the years to apply all I learned to help these systems grow in every way.

I learned about life including patience, love, and compassion from my wife and two children whom I owe more than anyone. Every year our relationships grew stronger with the continuum of one family staying together. I learned to care for children of every age because I raised two of my own. I learned to coach young new hires because I knew what motivated my own kids as they got older and entered the workforce. I learned how to care for a mother because I was married to the best. My wife helped me understand my own motivations and listen to my inner self-guidance, follow my own path to perform the best I could in anything I did.

I am nothing without my best friend and love of my life, Kim. She has been there with me from the beginning. I could have included more of our partnership through the book, of which she was an inspirational and integral part, but it had to be about the patients, and I cherish our privacy. Without her patience, understanding, and full support I could not have done the work I so needed to do. Living the life of a full time medic, committed to your calling, and working unending hours requires support. I'm not being dramatic when I say it can be a hard life, not only for me but for her. Working long shifts, sometimes 72 to 96 plus hours a week, dealing with insanity and death takes its toll. Coming home to an empty house after a week like that would be depressing if it was not for her. She lights up a room with her smile and taught me work-life balance; and life comes first. Who could be more inspirational and motivating?

Fortunately, I met Kim when I was a medic student in college. I was working full time as an orderly in the emergency room and performing my medic internship rounds in the ER when we met. Kim was doing her ER time for her college EMT course for experience and we bumped into each other at a code. Not very romantic but practical. As I worked and went through school she supported my efforts with encouragement every step of the way. After long shifts, I would vent about the tougher calls I had, not realizing that wasn't healthy for her or our relationship. I was on a shoestring budget and lived in a mobile home park. It was a nice park but it wasn't Park Avenue either—or what she deserved. She could see what she was getting into, but as her dad said, "She must be following her heart." Through my whole career, she has been there for me, and I do not believe I could have done it without her. The sanctity of our marriage helped form our own enduring characteristics that were applicable in all aspects of our lives. Those characteristics included unity, trust, honesty, respect and a devotion to care unceasingly. I learned as a husband who I am and how much I can care in a moment and for life. It is not a passive position but the most important proactive job. I avow the "sacredness" of it, not just "the marriage" on paper. It takes awareness of one's spirituality to understand that real commitment, devotion, or sacrifice are limited without it. For those hesitant on *commitment*, know there is great freedom in that, from yourself. Once again, my relationship with my wife helped make me who I am. Spirituality and faith made the difference in my life.

I spent a much of my adult life studying not only my religion but others in theology. I read the Christian and Hebrew Bibles (English translation). I worked on my church education committee with my wife, daughters, and fellow parishioners. I have respectfully researched and tried to understand what I could about all religions mentioned including passages and teachings from the Torah (English translation from Hebrew) and from the Quran (English translation from Arabic). I respect all faiths for what I had access to. I have sat in libraries trying to comprehend all I could and talked to as many people as I could about the spirituality of other cultures from the Native Americans to the far Eastern theologies. I am not a theologian (or omnist) but just one person trying to assist all in a growing sea of diversity.

The snapshot of examples I gave here were my attempts to *try* to help others in life and continue to this day.

To build successful communities in true unity we must work hard and that takes perseverance. The end of the great divide between the medical community and your town can be bridged by all including EMS personnel. This will take efforts from *everyone* including leaders in the community. I have shown there is room to learn about different theologies and discuss their patient care concepts within EMS. We don't have to be experts or become someone we are not; just listen, understand and assist. Maybe this could contribute to the start of those conversations.

It is the perseverance of my patients that was most inspirational.

What added to all these experiences was the training my patients gave me. It was through their beliefs and challenges at some of the worst moments of their lives, or end of their lives, that I learned to so respect and discover the spirituality of every human being. If they could endure their illness, suffering, and challenges in the face of death; so could I help them. That's what set me apart on this journey and made me a good medic. These people also helped me find out who I am deep in my soul. I am forever grateful that I was allowed to care and be there for people in need, for a newborn's first look, or a person's last look at this world. I was there for spiritual support, to fight the good fight, for them.

Thomas Valentini

APPENDIX

Christians were certainly the largest religious population in the areas I worked in New England; usually over fifty percent but it ranged. There are multiple denominations including but not limited to: Roman Catholic, Protestant, Greek and Russian Orthodox, Mormons, Jehovah's Witnesses, and Christian Scientists. Most of us know Christianity as the monotheistic religion based on the teachings of Jesus Christ. The old and new testaments of the Christian Bible are the accessible holy text used as a guide to lead a moral life through God's teachings. Christians believe they will be reunited with loved ones in the afterlife in Heaven. Christians believe there is a need for spiritual care at the end of life and understand that science and technology are not going to relieve all the suffering during death. That said some don't believe in the use of pain relief.

Christians believe in conducting end of life prayers: Last Rites are performed before death as it is approaching; the Eucharist (Holy Communion), which Christians receive throughout their life, is given one last time; and Anointing of the Sick is given as part of the Viaticum (in Catholicism) before death. A funeral is conducted at a church usually within seven days after death. The Christian community is close and rely on each other for support during the death of a loved one. If a medic or healthcare provider is needed by the patient they are given access and assistance. Often family will be present but not every Christian has the need to be surrounded as some believe there is no death alone with Jesus.

Judaism is the monotheistic religion of the ancient Hebrews. The Jewish people believe in one transcendent God found in the Torah, the 613 Mitzvot Commandments (first five books of Moses), the Halakha (religious laws based on the Torah), the Old Testament of the Bible, and the teachings of the rabbis (Talmud). They believe in one God who revealed himself to Abraham, Moses, and the Hebrew prophets and leading a life guided by scriptures and rabbinic laws and traditions with cultural influence. They value life and believe that death is the will of God. There are variations (Orthodox, Conservative, Reform) and so there are observant Jewish people whose decisions are balanced with consult from their Rabbi.

The medic on scene for the Jewish patient will find strict beliefs and practices guiding the end-of-life process. If not potentially curative, prolonging life in the terminally ill is typically refused, but sustaining life and healing can be promoted, based on the status of the patient's condition. Usually moving a patient at this time is also forbidden; we wouldn't touch the patient until advised, usually by the Rabbi and family. Relief of pain and discomfort is allowed as long as it doesn't hasten death.

When a patient dies the family may position them supine, cover them with a white sheet, and attend the deceased for 20-30 minutes. The deceased are often prepared by friends and family immediately after death for the burial and within 24 hours as per their law.

Islam is the second largest religion in the world with 1.8 billion followers. The numbers where I worked were small but present and growing. The monotheistic religion of the Muslims teaches that there is only one God and that the prophet Muhammed is the messenger of God (Allah). Islamic law is not Sharia law. I have been told Sharia law is based more on their holy books' divine code and philosophical guidance. This includes the precepts of Islam, the holy book Qur'an (the recitation), and the Hadith (traditions.) There are many diverse traditions that are accepted due to social, demographic, denominational, and cultural variations.

Muslims view life on earth as a preparation for eternal life. Although mourning is visible for a three day period, they may express joy that the deceased is at peace with Allah. I am told some prefer to die at home with children and family members around them. They may continue to pray five times a day. At the last moments of life, an Imam may be requested by family to guide prayers or rituals. Family members may take turns reading the Quran at the bedside. A close family member may encourage Talqeen, urging the dying person to recite the Islamic declaration of faith known as the Shahada. This is important for the dying to achieve a "good death." Cremation is forbidden, and burial takes place as soon as possible. Family members maintain bedside vigil during end of life care and at the time of death. If healthcare providers are needed they will be given brief access with respect to the patient.

Buddhism is the world's fourth largest religion with over 500 million followers. Buddha (meaning "Awakened One" in Sanskrit) is also known as Siddhartha Gautama and is neither a God nor deity. He was a teacher who lived in northern India between the mid-6th to mid-4th centuries BCE and had a spiritual awakening at the age of 35. Buddhist sacred texts were passed down orally by Buddhist monastics and collected into Buddhist scriptures known as the Pali canon.

The basic teachings of Buddha are the three universal truths: 1) everything is impermanent and changing; 2) impermanence leads to suffering, making life imperfect; and 3) the self is not personal and unchanging. By following the path of Buddha to enlightenment, the individual can dispel the ignorance that perpetuates suffering. This is the first of four noble truths: 1) human life has suffering; 2) the cause is greed; 3) there is an end to suffering; and 4) the way to end suffering is to follow the middle path. The middle path is the path to Nirvana (a state of Enlightenment).

There is the Noble Eightfold path or middle way between exxtremes of asceticism and sensual indulgance. I will not list the eight elements here but these qualities are present in those who understand Nirvana. He rejected the soul as a metaphysical substance, though recognized the existence of self as the subject of action in a practical and moral sense. He taught methods for defeating our negative minds (anger, jealousy, ignorance) and developing our positive thoughts such as love, compassion, and wisdom.

Buddhists recognize death and grief are universal. Reincarnation is a central theme within Buddhist philosophy. Death is the beginning of a new life, not the end of life. Personal and significant items are placed around the coffin. Meditation by the dying person is common and is described as the art of dying consciously and peacefully. There are variations in burial, but funerals are said to be kept simple. Embalming and cremation are acceptable within most Buddhist customs.

Hinduism is the ancient religious and cultural tradition of South Asia with about 1.25 billion followers. Hindus believe in one God, Brahman (the Supreme Over Soul from whom all creation comes from), but in different manifestations. The precepts were set in scripture known as the Vedas (c. 1,500-500 BCE) but orally long before. Hinduism scripture (like all scripture) is too complex to go into detail here, but the philosophy is inspiring. The range of beliefs and practices in end of life care and suffering appears to have many variables not guided directly by scripture.

I've read and try to understand that Hindus:

"Believe in a oneness of existence with the higher aspect of self (Atman) as part of everyone's self as well as the Over Soul/Mind and following one's duty in life (dharma) with proper action (karma), to evade the bonds of physical existence and escape from the cycle of rebirth (reincarnation) and death (samsara). Once the individual has done that, the Atman joins with Brahman and one has returned home to primordial oneness...The soul is immortal, has always existed as part of Brahman and will always exist – therefore the finality of death is an illusion. At death, Hindu's believe the soul discards the body and is reincarnated if it failed to attain Moksha or, if it did, the Atman becomes one with Brahman and returns to its eternal home. *(Joshua J. Mark)*

While I find Hinduism fascinating and respect their beliefs and practices as others, I haven't had as much experience with it because the population of this religious culture were small where I worked. Thus, my experiences are limited here.

They believe suffering and illness can be seen as the result of prior actions in this or a past life, as result of karma. The Hindu patient may refuse pain relief to consciously focus their mind on God. Hindus do believe in a "good death" that they are prepared for at the right place and time if possible. The elders seek to conclude their responsibilities in this life and may make visits to their temple for prayers and offerings. The family may recite mantras and Hindu prayers during the patient's last moments. At the of end-of-life care we have been called only to pronounce death so that they may make funeral arrangements, usually within 24 hours after death. Hindus usually desire a natural death and not prolonging it with medical or mechanical interventions that may interfere with the soul's karma passing from this life to the next life. So, comfort care DNRs are sometimes present on scene. Family members are often close and involved with making end-of-life care decisions.

Agnostic and Atheist. These are not a religion but certainly a group of individuals. Agnostics believe that nothing is known of the existence or nature of God or anything beyond the material phenomena; a person who claims neither faith nor disbelief in God. Atheists do not believe in the existence of God or anything divine and think it is all a speculative hypothesis. As I mentioned, this demographic comprises over 23% of some communities, such as those I worked in (Association of Religious Data Archives).

End of life care for this group is based on the individual and their preferences. Depending on location and cultural influences, some identify as Atheist or Agnostic, then a small percentage will identify as Humanists, Spiritual, Pagan, Buddhist in Nature, Nontheistic, Apatheist, Gnostic, or None. In my experience, most are not concerned with any ceremonial process. I have experienced and read that some are concerned with assistance in dying so that they don't suffer unnecessarily or are uncomfortable in those last moments. Others are concerned with "death with dignity," so having their bed made or their surroundings in order is a concern. I've had some wish for family or friends present and funeral arrangements to be overseen. Most appreciate assistance and all we need to do is ask.